YIELD TO JOY

YIELD TO JOY

The Miraculous Power
of Forgiveness

PAMELA WHITMAN

DreamSculpt
MEDIA + BOOKS

ISBN-13: 978-1-949003-33-8 print edition
ISBN-13: 978-1-949003-34-5 ebook edition

Photograph of Pamela Whitman by Paul Dempsey

First printing edition 2020

Waterside Productions

DreamSculpt Books
Waterside Productions, Inc.
2055 Oxford Avenue
Cardiff, CA 92007

To the loving memory of Allyn S. Lehman,
who demonstrated consistent humility and love.

ACKNOWLEDGMENTS

My heartfelt gratitude goes out to the following people:

My family and friends for surrounding me with love and support. I am truly blessed.

The *Course in Miracles* community. You inspire me every day.

Aldona Middlesworth for your editorial talent and being a loyal advocate of my ministry.

Chris Souchak for your steadfast encouragement. Your faith in this book helped keep the momentum going.

Toby Bridson for your renderings of the stick figures and Ojedokun Daniel O. for the cover design.

Jared Rosen at DreamSculpt Books for the direction and opportunity.

Josh Freel and everyone at Waterside Productions for your dedication and professionalism.

Thanks be to God.
Amen

TABLE OF CONTENTS:

INTRODUCTION

I saw God. It was *not* a near-death experience. My body did not undergo a coma, car accident or fever. It was a near-*life* experience. A group of us were enjoying some rockin' Indian food. I had just eaten a perfect vegetable samosa. As often happens in large, lively groups, multiple discussions bounced around the table simultaneously. My attention shifted casually from one conversation to another. As I turned my head, my eyes rested on a laughing lady whose name I do not know. With no effort and absolutely no warning, I popped out of time and space. I was *in* the Love of God. I communed with the most powerful love of my life, *multiplied by* infinity *plus* eternity. Love and I existed as one unlimited Self. We weren't separate from anything or anyone. No dead relatives came bearing greetings. The perception of the realm of bodies had disappeared. There *was* white light with little sparkles of color, but no tunnel. This Jersey girl *merged* without traffic or tolls!

Even during this direct experience of God, part of my mind held out. This is the part of my mind I had to forgive. Self-forgiveness is a plan and a process. During the revelation experience, the resistant mind (ego) tried to figure out what was happening. The Inner Teacher spoke too. Some of you call that Voice "Holy Spirit" or "Higher Power." Whenever the resistant mind offered an intellectual explanation for the experience, Holy Spirit said, "No, that's not it." The Holy Spirit was quiet and respectful. Not the ego. Oh, no! It eventually figured out what was happening and panicked. It started ordering me back. "Don't go! Come back!" Suddenly, I noticed the laughing lady staring at me oddly. She started explaining the joke. I acted as if I had not just directly encountered God. I ate another samosa.

After the revelation experience, I began to perceive anything other than love as resistance. It became easy to see through it. I want to go back to Heaven and want everyone to join in the direct encounter with God. None of us can get there by ourselves. We each have a part to play in bringing us all back to the garden. Our job is to become ready by being willing. God has the whole program planned out for us. (We are in the process of *remembering* wholeness.) Our part is small but mighty. It's like the samosa at an Indian dinner—essential! As we let go of our armed resistance to God and learn to trust the Inner Teacher, we accept our part. We are given earth plane steps that always end up having something to do with forgiveness. Our willingness to forgive undoes our resistance to happiness.

A Course in Miracles is my preferred manual for this process. It suits me with its musical poetry and undogmatic God-Love-Beauty. The Inner Teacher knows my style. One day I prayed for a book that would stretch me. The book moved from a shelf in one part of my house to a chair in my bedroom. How did that happen? I called, and it came. (I didn't even have to give it a treat.) With the permission of Course in Miracles Society (CIMS), I will quote some favorite passages to you from *A Course in Miracles The Original Edition*. These quotes will look like this: ACIM Chapter.Section. Paragraph.

A Course in Miracles uses male pronouns. For a while, that bugged me. Every time I came upon a male pronoun in *The Course*, I changed it to feminine. I would show *them*! (You can show them too if it makes you happy.) Eventually, the "Pronoun Equality Liberation Army" revealed itself to be the ego's way of distracting me from the message of *The Course*. The joy of God became more important than making "them" wrong about words.

(Hint: foreshadowing.)

Let's start now.

Do you want joy?

Take several deep cleansing breaths.

Now—allow yourself to question your belief that joy isn't here already.

Permit yourself to question your thoughts.

Your mind has just opened.

Opt for the Essence

The Road to Joy

For a decade and a half, I led my band WorldColor in national tours. It was very orderly. Agents scheduled concerts almost a year in advance. There were airlines, itineraries, comfortable hotels and an occasional limo. I could see the future and knew what to expect. WorldColor promoted world peace through inter-cultural understanding. We played original rock and traditional music from the countries represented in the group. Audiences learned about the beauty of world cultures though our multi-media concerts. For a few years, Japanese was the primary language in the group, but we all "spoke" music.

The band was based in Los Angeles, but the musicians had immigrated from all over the globe. Many of them came to the United States to study rock at the Musicians Institute in Hollywood. When we needed a new band member, I would call their placement department to find applicants for the audition. My answering machine would fill up with exotic foreign accents. Some applicants left rock riffs over the phone along with their contact information. When a cast member changed, the show would reflect the new country represented in the band. We played in performing arts centers, colleges, schools, Indian Reservations and nontraditional venues. After each tour, I would review. "What did I learn on this tour?" Eventually, I had it down to a system, a routine. Because I had learned well from that form of the situation, change was on the horizon.

At Christmas, I visited my brother who was living in Kathmandu, Nepal. The city of one and a half million people, countless stray dogs, scampering monkeys and sacred cows was alive with music. Temple bells rang through air weighted with pollution and incense. We could hear the city awaken each morning as hawkers began selling their wares and traffic sang with a cacophony of horns and bells from bicycle rickshaws. At the top of the Swayambhunath Stupa (known by visitors as the Monkey Temple), American funk music played on a portable CD player while inside the temple, Buddhist monks chanted and blew into long ceremonial horns. We met several Nepalese musicians. The experience inspired me to deepen the level of WorldColor's cultural exchange by recruiting musicians from Nepal to join the band. There were no openings in my concert schedule until the next fall. I thought, *"If I don't have any bookings in the fall, I will come back to Kathmandu."*

Back in the United States, WorldColor's agent booked a fall tour. A prominent television show hired our guitarist to be in the house band. I hired a new guitarist and took new band photos. A friend looked at the photo and delivered a message. She said the band would disappear and I would be a soloist. I would have everything I had ever *really* wanted. (At the time, I did not appreciate this message.)

Another television show hired the new guitarist. For the first time, the concert presenters canceled the fall tour. The reason the concert presenters gave for the cancellation was untrue. I heard an echo in my heart, *"If I don't have a tour in the fall, I'll go back to Kathmanduuuuuu."* The Universe was clearing my schedule. In October, I flew back to Nepal in search of a guitarist. I didn't know it was the beginning of a three-year cultural exchange program with the Himalayan Kingdom. It would be the culmination of WorldColor and a change in direction for my career.

"What could you not accept if you but knew that everything that happens, all events, past, present, and to come, are gently planned by One Whose only purpose is your good?"
ACIM. Workbook. Lesson.135.19

My first day back in Kathmandu, I appeared on Nepali television and met more new friends. The annual celebration of Tihar (Festival of Lights) was in full swing. Houses were decorated with illumined clay lanterns welcoming the Hindu gods and goddesses. Colorful ceremonial dyes marked foreheads of the celebrants and even the furry foreheads of dogs on Dog Honoring Day. There were flower garlands, prayers, music and themes for each day of the five-day festival. It was a joy to be part of the celebration.

After the bustle of the festival, my traveling companion and I headed to Pokhara to relax. Pokhara is Nepal's second stop for most visitors to the country. Its slower pace offers fewer cars and more cows. The popular Lakeside district serves as a base for trekkers hiking the Annapurna Circuit of the Himalayas or vacationers wanting to enjoy the natural beauty of Phewa Lake. The Lake reflects the Himalayas and provides a peaceful environment for floating in a rowboat or paddling to the far side and climbing to the world peace pagoda. My friend settled into the leisurely lifestyle in

Pokhara. After a trek and visiting with friends in Lakeside, I returned to Kathmandu to get to work.

Sitting alone in the Hotel White Lotus in Kathmandu, it dawned on me that I had traveled halfway around the world with a big idea and exactly one contact in the Nepalese music industry. Panic set in. *What was I thinking?!* But I didn't have to choose fear. I could choose peace instead.

> *"I can elect to change all thoughts that hurt."*
> *ACIM.Workbook.Lesson.284*

I did not push the fear down, nor did I visualize guitarists, tours or concerts. Sitting on my bed, I remembered I had come in service of peace. I called upon the feelings of joy and peace that are always available. The joy and peace within are not dependent on any specific outcome. In that moment, I was not 7,500 miles from home, but dwelling in my *eternal* home—the peace and joy of God. Using the phone in the hotel lobby, I called my one contact. We met, and I learned he was a record company owner at the center of Nepal's music industry. He introduced me to promoters, press, and radio and television stations.

I began collaborating with a trio that had recently won the Nepalese version of the Grammy Awards. By playing a benefit concert for women and children, I met more members of the press. Without effort, I was handed a platform of radio, television, documentaries, recordings, performances and press that kept coming as long as I stayed. *So I stayed* for three years! I made lasting relationships. Half way around the globe, I found people I would know and love for the rest of my life. I brought Nepalese musicians to tour the United States as members of WorldColor and brought WorldColor to tour Nepal. WorldColor became a sensation in the Himalayan Kingdom. Reporters asked, *"What is your message for Nepal?"* I was given the opportunity to speak about peace and love to large audiences.

The Himalayan Broadcasting Company offered me a weekly radio show based on *A Course in Miracles.* It occurred to me that broadcast was more efficient than touring. I didn't have to take my body around to the people. All I had to do was talk into the microphone about inner peace. The message traveled *for* me. When it was time to come back to the United States, it was also time to let go of WorldColor. All of our lives shifted at the same time. We had completed our assignment joyfully.

My Inner Teacher directed me, "Await further instructions." At first, I pretended I did not know what to do and tried to think of something myself. I made up plans and told myself they were for God. They were not. I could have called them "Music for Impatience"; "The Forcing Solutions Tour"; "Playing for Fear of Change." None of these projects brought the experience of inner peace. They showed me my choice for an old form at the expense of the *content* of Peace. When we choose form over content, we are turning away from our Source and forgetting Who Created Us.

The joy of WorldColor had not come from touring, but from doing God's Will. The idea for WorldColor had come to me in a vision during meditation. A Native American friend brought the rest of the instructions about the band. By following God's Will in the world of form, we experience the joy and peace that is the Will we share with God. When we want peace, we follow the Spirit of Peace. I was learning that Inner Peace was what I wanted above all else.

The plans I made to resist letting go of the past blocked the experience of peace inside. They were a defense against the experience of my True Relationship with God. Our Relationship with God is the experience of love, joy and peace. I recognized it wasn't touring I missed; it was peace, and I wanted it back. My mistaken plans became the motivation to practice the lessons from the workbook of *A Course in Miracles* with great dedication. Five minutes of meditation at the top of every hour became my lifeline. Spirit had told me what to do: *wait.* Through meditation, I learned to sit, stay and heal. Life without an outer project was good for me. Consistently turning to the peace of God within prepared me for my next assignment in the world. The Inner Teacher is so smart. After I relaxed into not touring, the next assignment from Spirit appeared.

"Some of your greatest advances you have judged as failures, and some of your deepest retreats you have evaluated as success."

ACIM.18.VI.41

The next assignment did not include a group, the performing arts circuit, airlines or the structures I had known. For three years, I would travel up and down the East Coast, driving to spiritual centers, hippie style. When I dedicated my career to God with great enthusiasm, I didn't know my career would change form many times.

As we advance on our spiritual journey, we learn to *value content over form.* We value joy, love, and peace because those are all names for God. Any time we make a U-turn and value form above content, we are giving ourselves the potential for a grievance. We are choosing the bumpy road. Through experience, we learn to let our Inner Teacher show the way and meet our needs. We learn this in an orderly fashion. Our Teacher has a Plan that reflects our willingness to heal. As forgiveness clears our minds of fear thoughts, the outside world shifts. People are sent to us and we are sent to them. The Plan will match us with people and situations selected to advance our understanding. The assignments further the spiritual development of all involved.

As form changes, our lives can look temporarily disorganized. The Plan is well-ordered; our minds are not. Our unloving thoughts rise to the surface to be forgiven. We learn to trust the process; to have faith in the One Who Is *really* in charge. The trust is the healing. Learning to look to our Inner Guide is how we forgive. All of our unloving thoughts reveal past resistance to love, resurfacing to be undone. We are so loved that we are given an opportunity to see those thoughts and hand them over. Following the Guidance of Spirit in our lives builds our certainty. It's how we recognize the unconditional love that's here for us. It's safe to be honest about our blooper thoughts and mistakes. We are healing our relationship with an Eternal Love that never left.

"We are therefore embarking on an organized, well structured, and carefully planned program aimed at learning how to offer to the Holy Spirit everything you do not want."
ACIM.Text.11.3.23

Before setting out on the first of these tours, I turned within and asked, "Am I meant to go on this tour?" I waited for an answer. (Progress!) Divine signs showed up, and a helper appeared. Spirit had sent another courageous and willing soul. Roadie Jim and I packed the Honda and drove south. We agreed that we would: 1. Not share a bedroom. 2. Not sleep in the car. We would follow Divine Guidance, sure our needs would be met.

In this new incarnation of touring, the itineraries often shifted around en route. Some venues provided a guest room or couch in a private home on the night of the event. On many nights, we did not know in advance where we would stay. My trust was being developed. I was shifting my faith away from planning and giving my trust to a Higher Plan. We learn that faith in the Universal Happiness Plan is justified by making the leap.

At the time, I prayed every day for God to bless everyone in the world. I said the prayer for years. Now I say a different form of the prayer. Like everything else, the content remains, while the form reflects my current understanding. The prayer helped me recognize I already loved people when I met them. Wherever we traveled, I met people from my prayers. It was a joy! I was not seeing strangers, but Loved ones. It was like a family reunion at every turn.

"He sees no strangers, only dearly loved and loving friends."
ACIM.20.3.9

I gave lectures, concerts, and forgiveness workshops at churches, synagogues and yoga studios. We noticed that our assignments included encounters at restaurants, gas stations, in each place and every moment. *A Course in Miracles* says that we are all teaching, all the time. We are always demonstrating love or fear. The places we stayed and people we met were part of the Universal Happiness Plan. Some people delivered messages for us. Other times we had messages for them. Sometimes old unforgiveness would reveal itself in order to be undone.

Roadie Jim sold my CDs at the events and we always had enough money to keep going. Sometimes we ended up in a modest hotel where The Plan gave us opportunities to let go of our unforgiving thoughts. One day after a long stretch of driving, we pulled into a humble establishment and started to unload the equipment. I had the first floor room and Roadie Jim checked in upstairs. As we were moving the music gear into my room, a truck full of road workers used their eyes and mouths to greet me with sexual aggression. The energy shook me up. I locked the door to my room and sat down. It sounded raucous next door and outside of my room. I asked Spirit what to do. The thought came, "Pray for them." I had prayed for them daily as part of my "everyone in the world" prayer. It was time to pray for them for the second time that day.

"When a brother acts insanely, he is offering you an opportunity to bless him. His need is yours. You need the blessing you can offer him. There is no way for you to have it except by giving it. This is the law of God, and it has no exceptions."

ACIM.7.8.72

I prayed for them with my whole heart. Next, I extended the prayer and sent blessings to everyone who had ever behaved in sexually inappropriate ways. *Then it happened.* I realized the love I felt for someone I had been praying to forgive. I started to laugh and cry tears of joy and release at the same time. "Holy Spirit, you tricked me because you wanted me to let go of that grievance! Thank you!" Holy

Spirit hadn't tricked me. Willingness to heal brought the opportunity to let go of my unloving thought. The situation was an answer to prayer. Spirit always answers our prayers. We receive the answer when we are willing to accept the *content*. The Universal Happiness Plan had given me another chance to bless and this time I chose love. I made the choice to recognize inappropriate behavior as a call for love, and extended it. Love, peace and joy returned to my awareness. My heart healed in a motel behind a Waffle House off the highway. The noise outside subsided just as the inner disturbance left my heart. The yoga center called and offered a place for us to stay the next night.

While far from home and dog for months at a time, it helped to remember the love of God surrounded me. I never felt lonely. Even when Roadie Jim moved away after the first two years, I felt deeply connected. While barreling down the highway, I would bless the other drivers as I passed each car, or as they passed me. My connection to Guidance was heightened because I was aware I needed it. The old way didn't work anymore. Roadie Jim taught me to practice testing out the "Lilies of the Field" theory. It gave me confidence. He stayed until I was ready to fly solo. When I left a town with no idea where I would stay that night, I never said, "I don't have a place to stay." Instead, I said, "I don't know where I am staying *yet*." I answered the Call and all resources necessary were provided.

My treks in the Himalayas had been practice. When trekking the Annapurna range, we would hike until sunset. When the sun started to go down, villagers would come to the trail and offer us shelter. I didn't know I was in training for tours that would come later. Spirit showed up all over the world, blessing my every step.

I was in the ordination program at the time of the Southern driving tours, so I would call San Francisco to attend classes from the road. There was a stretch in Florida where I had no bookings and did not know where I would stay (yet) for several days. I spread out the map and wondered whom I would connect with for those few days. I opened my *A Course in Miracles* book "randomly" and found a business card. *(How did it get there?)* It was the card of a woman who supported the performing arts. She moved to Florida years before and came to a concert in New Jersey that summer during a vacation. With her business card in my hand I remembered the moment she handed it to me. *"If you are ever in Florida and need a place to stay, call me."*

We enjoyed a wonderful visit. We attended the Florida Orchestra, who performed a major work for flute. My host told me stories about her friend who traveled for his work and stayed with her when in the area. She said he had passed away at her house. I ducked into her guest room to call my ordination class. After the class, she asked about the denomination. When I told her, *"A Course in Miracles,"* she said, "I love *A Course in Miracles!*" Our conversation shifted to a whole new level. She related that her traveling friend was a medium, at which point she delivered a long message for my life.

As the journey continued, I started hearing messages about suicide. It was not about me. It didn't seem to be about anyone in my daily life. Frequently, I would turn on the radio just as a public service announcement about suicide prevention was broadcasting. There were stories in the news about an athlete who had taken his life. These images were standing out and catching my attention. The Plan led me to the home of a woman who offered shelter to travelers.

As soon as I walked in her door, she told me of her sorrow. She explained that she was preparing to take her own life. I saw the means she was planning to use. She was serious.

It was an assignment.

This was another step for me in learning to follow Spirit's Guidance. I had no intention of giving unsolicited advice. "Helping" is not the same as being Truly Helpful. Good intentions of "helping" are a defense against the Universal Plan. But I remembered what the *Course* says. I could be Truly Helpful by letting the Holy Spirit speak through me. The Holy Spirit had faith in me to listen and follow. I would let my body be a communication device for the same Higher Wisdom that had led me to this woman's door. The Holy Spirit would give me the words.

I listened for the words and spoke. The woman did not like the words. She insisted she had lost the source of her happiness. The pain was so great that she planned to end it by committing suicide. I went to bed in one of her guest rooms and had intense dreams. In the morning, the Holy Spirit gave me more words, and I spoke them. The woman received the message and had a breakthrough! She let go of her pain and found a way back to her True Source. We embraced. While holding her body in my arms, I glanced over her shoulder. On her refrigerator was this quote from *A Course in Miracles*:

> *"I am here only to be Truly Helpful. I am here to represent Christ, Who sent me. I do not have to worry about what to say or what to do because He Who sent me will direct me. I*

am content to be wherever He wishes, knowing he goes there
with me. I will be healed as I let Him teach me to heal. "

ACIM. 7.8.72

Later that day, I sat meditating. I didn't miss the structured tours with guaranteed paychecks, comfortable hotels, lighting plots, and outward "security." The past *form* of a relationship had dropped from my mind. By choosing to follow Spirit, I found the enduring joy within. Gratitude filled my heart. The experience of serving and being used by my True Protection was incomparable. I was not asking God for anything; not even asking God to bless anyone; but sending thanks. "Thank You... Thank You... Thank You..." Suddenly I heard, "Thank *You.*"

Yielding to our reliance on Spirit deepens our ability to hear and accept the Eternal Truth. Spirit encourages us to choose the *content* of joy, love and peace. The message will come through us and to us. The form of the delivery doesn't matter because the Teacher is the joy, love and peace emanating from the Source we all share. Our relationship to Source strengthens because of our willingness to listen and follow. Turning to Spirit moment by moment is the Road to Joy. It's the Road to Living as the Self God Created.

LEARN TO TRUST THE
HIGHER PLAN

GANDHI ALLOWED HIS MIND TO BE TRAINED

According to Hinduism, Krishna was a flute god. (You've got to love Hindu people!) Krishna said, "There is nothing wrong with the mind that training will not cure." *A Course in Miracles* says, *"An untrained mind can accomplish nothing"* (ACIM.Workbook.Introduction.1). Our mind training is speeding up. We are awakening to the Truth that we are One. This acceleration *is* the opening of the mind.

As we heal, the outside world reflects the changes stirring within. On the surface level, it looks as if jobs and entire industries are disappearing right off the planet. But there is a big opening in the Mind Department. The healing happens in the Mind and then shines outward. Our real job is the same for everyone. You won't find it listed on any employment sites, but the function of the job will be the same in every circumstance. Our function is forgiveness. Forgiveness reveals our love, peace and joy.

Our minds heal by forgiving our unloving thoughts. This requires a process of re-training. Even Gandhi changed careers. He enjoyed experimentation and even called his autobiography, *My Experiments with Truth*. Gandhi was always growing and allowing his mind to be trained. If you read two things he wrote, and they conflicted, he said to go with what he had written more recently. He developed an evolving philosophy by studying other points of view and conducting experiments on himself.

Gandhi was not attached to a fixed point of view. He didn't say, "The train stops here!" He had the courage to let his mind be changed. In his autobiography, he wrote, "I hope and pray that no one will regard the advice as authoritative. The experiments narrated should be regarded as illustrations, in the light of which everyone may carry on his (or her) own experiments according to his (or her) own inclinations and capacity." (I added the "hers.") Whenever we declare, "The train has stopped; I know everything," we become unteachable. When we stagnate, we will not experience new landscapes of the mind.

Delay causes pain.
Pain is not our True Will.

In 1893 in South Africa, the young attorney Mohandas Gandhi took a train ride. When he entered the first-class compartment that day, he presumed the train ride was a business trip for a case he was working on.

But we never know what anything is for.

We don't perceive our best interests because we don't understand Who We Are. Our decision to identify with a separate, little self, with separate little interests prevents us from knowing anything. We assume everything that is happening is about us, "little us," "body us" with our little beliefs about what will make us happy. (These beliefs seem to be big and important!) But we don't perceive the Source of our Happiness. Our beliefs about what will make us happy (separate from everyone else in the world) are judgments. Judgments are violent thoughts.

Gandhi's life wound up being about nonviolence. When we believe we recognize what we need in order to be happy in our separate life, we are BLOCKING our awareness of the Universal, PERFECT PLAN for everyone's Happiness. Gandhi boarded the train and did not understand why. Until we know that everything is for love, peace and joy, we don't remember why we are doing anything. (Gandhi assumed it was about a lawsuit.)

A Caucasian man entered the compartment on the train and noticed Gandhi sitting there. The Caucasian man saw a separate body with different skin color. He pre-judged Gandhi. The man used a small part of his brain to project violent thoughts toward Gandhi. He also used his mouth. The man demanded that Gandhi leave the first-class compartment.

"Those who see themselves as whole make no demands."
ACIM Workbook Lesson 37

Gandhi said, "No." Sometimes the word, "No," is the Truth. He had a first-class ticket and understood that he was not "less-than" this Caucasian man. Gandhi did not perceive a body that was "more-than" and a body that was "less-than." He did not leave. Then the police came. The police saw separation. They tossed Gandhi off the train and onto the platform. They beat Gandhi's body and used their mouths to speak insulting words. Gandhi was afraid, but he did not want to stay that way. He prayed and asked for Divine Guidance.

"Prayer is the medium of miracles. Prayer is the natural communication of the created with the Creator."

ACIM 1.1 Miracle Principle 1

Gandhi did not try to solve the problem alone. He gave the problem to the Divine. *A Course in Miracles* tells us, *"To give a problem to the Holy Spirit to solve for you means that you want it solved. To keep it for yourself to solve without His help is to decide it should remain unsettled, unresolved, and lasting in its power of injustice and attack."* (25.X.84)

When Gandhi prayed, the Plan moved forward. He met some Indian people who gave him support. He spent the night in Standerton, talking with his new friends. They discussed the problem of prejudice in South Africa. Gandhi remembered that he was a lawyer. He was very effective at using *his* mouth to convince people. The next day he rode another train. Guess what—it was a bigger train, with a bigger compartment. When he arrived at his destination, Gandhi was given a bigger platform. He started holding regular public gatherings, giving speeches about equality and nonviolence.

The man on the train was a trainer. On the surface level, it looked like the man on the train was a *big, fat ego.* He was a "bad guy" who was being really mean to our "hero," Gandhi. This is how it looks if we view our story through the eyes of separation. We are very accustomed to using these eyes. (Therefore, we need training.) There is only One Will. God's Will is done. The Universal Happiness Plan is always on track. The man on the train was part of the Universal

Happiness Plan. He served the Mind Training of many people throughout time and space. The "hero" in our storyline helped to speed up our training by asking for Divine Guidance and following it. The training is always in motion. It *accelerates* when we put it into the Hands of the One Who Knows the Whole Plan.

If Gandhi had stayed *down* on the platform in Standerton, crying and thinking about his little, small "self-interests"— his business trip, his wounded pride—would he have moved forward to a bigger platform in that moment? Would he have been a "hero" at all? He asked for Divine Help. The Universal Hand helped Gandhi to stand up in Standerton. Gandhi stood up so he could keep progressing. He did not deny his feelings. He paused and noticed that his heart was racing.

Then he prayed.

Then he stood up and continued the training. He allowed for change. Gandhi gave the problem over in prayer. He prayed to God for help. His little separate interests were not what everything was about. When we hold on to our imaginary separate interests, we are refusing to let go of our identification with a separate self. By trusting Spirit with our lives, we learn to identify with the One Who cannot be separate. We learn that we are Whole. There is no loss in Wholeness. By practicing placing the situations of our lives in the Hands of Spirit, we serve the Whole Self.

Gandhi allowed the incident to open his Mind to something Universally Helpful. He began training others. Because he opened his Mind, he allowed others to be trained *through* him. Even now, others are being trained through Gandhi's

Real Thoughts. His body is no longer here. But Gandhi is still serving the Universal Happiness Plan. Gandhi's Real Thoughts influenced Martin Luther King Junior's strategies throughout the civil rights movement. Real Thoughts are Eternal because they come from God.

When Gandhi arrived in Pretoria, he gave his first public speech. It was the start of what was to become an international movement called Satyagraha (Love Force – Truth Firmness). *Satya* is a word derived from *sat*, which means "being." Gandhi wrote that, "Nothing is or exists in reality except truth. That is why Sat or truth is perhaps the most important name of God. In fact it is more correct to say that truth is God than to say God is truth." The *graha* part means "force" or "firmness." To allow our minds to accept the truth that nothing but God is real, that nothing other than love exists, we have to keep choosing loving thoughts. We have to practice firmness with our minds by sticking with the training.

Satyagraha is vigilance for truth. *A Course in Miracles* tells us that a major step in our mind training, our thought reversal is to *"be vigilant ONLY for God and HIS Kingdom."* (Chapter 6c) We have already been *really* vigilant. We are quite good at it. For billions of years we have practiced teaching ourselves impossible thoughts. Through repetition, we have used our powerful minds to teach ourselves that separation, lack, death and downright cruelty are real. We have taught ourselves that the Self God Created is little. And we actually *believe* this stuff. Just ask our emotions. Now our vigilance is changing direction to focus on the force of love. We have to "do reps," choosing again and again for the love of God that is the truth about us.

Gandhi led the people in South Africa in overcoming the pass laws of apartheid by using satyagraha. Apartheid meant apart-hate. Gandhi called upon the force that no illusion can resist. Love Force dissolved the illusion of hate, the illusion of separation. Satyagraha was a literal movement. It had momentum and swept India where Gandhi's followers overturned the British control using non-co-operation.

A Course in Miracles tells us, *"I rule my mind, which I alone must rule." The Course* is telling us, *"My mind can only serve. 6 Today I give its service to the Holy Spirit to employ as He sees fit. 7 I thus direct my mind, which I alone can rule. 8 And thus I set it free to do the Will of God"* (ACIM Workbook Lesson 236). When we give our mind to the Holy Spirit to rule, we are putting our kingdom under Divine Authority. In this way, we are serving love.

To serve love, we must remember we do not know what anything is for. There is a Universal Plan to bring forth the Happiness of all. Today we can serve the Universal Plan. Any plan we make, no matter how well-intentioned, is based on separation. Our self-initiated plans *are* little. We can't be in charge of the Universal Plan. We base our plans on separate sight; separate interests. We imagine separate interests because we believe we are little, separate selves. The Universal Plan heals our minds of separation thoughts as we learn to trust and follow the Mind of Wholeness.

There are NO separate interests because separation is not real. There is a Universal Force of Love that is moving everything in perfect coordination for the happiness of all because there really is One Self. We are being trained to see that. Our minds are being trained. Your mind is being trained. My mind is being trained. Gandhi's mind was being trained. Gandhi used various tactics as part of his campaign to overcome oppression though nonviolent methods. One of these methods was self-deprivation. He used *fasting*, hunger strikes to influence the people. When mill workers were waning in their commitment to a strike, Gandhi decided that he would not eat.

He said, *"Unless the strikers rally and continue the strike until a settlement is reached, or till they leave the mills altogether, I will not touch any food."* Gandhi forgot that he did not know the Whole Plan. He forgot "force" has more than one meaning. When we try to impose our separate will, we are seeing separation. With Gandhi's little body wasting away, some people felt too guilty to *not* do what he wanted them to do. He had good intentions. Gandhi was trying to help. Gandhi admitted that he had conflicted thoughts about this approach and that the outcomes were mixed. (Gandhi was thinking some Real Thoughts and some *nothing* thoughts. Sound familiar?)

"Perception is a mirror, not a fact. And what I look on is my state of mind reflected outward."
ACIM Workbook Lesson 304

During the 1970s grape boycott, Cesar Chavez followed Gandhi's fasting strategies to influence the farm workers in maintaining nonviolent resistance. Cesar Chavez implemented hunger strikes and lost lots of weight. People felt bad. It worked! Cesar Chavez was able to get people to do what he wanted them to do by depriving himself. This *seemed* to have a good effect. The grape pickers got a better contract. There was no *outer* violence. The mind training continued for everyone.

Then, Osho entered the scene.

Osho was an Indian mystic also known as Rajneesh. He was controversial and didn't care. Osho was into liberating the mind. The Mind Training was moving forward. (Choo! Choo!) Osho confronted the blocks to Truth. Osho pointed out that Gandhi was using guilt to manipulate people. OUCH! Whenever I read Osho, I first say, "HOW DARE HE WRITE THAT?!" and then, a moment later, "Huh?! It's true!" The Universal Happiness Plan does not include increasing the belief in illusion. Guilt is an illusion. The Plan is all about Happiness. It's a *Universal* Happiness Plan.

The ego says, "I know people who do that!"…Yes, there are people in my life who mirror my hidden agendas back to me to liberate me from *my* hidden thoughts. My plan won't work. Looking deeply, I admit I base my self-initiated plans on my agendas, *my judgments.* I base my plans on the little parts, the separate parts I can see. Therefore, I must remember I know nothing. I do not recognize what anything is for. I don't have the Whole perspective. Everything that is happening now, everything that will ever happen, everything that happened in the past was for the best interest, the Happiness of my Self. My Whole Self is everyone and everything. Everyone has an important part to play today for the Universal Plan. Now, I forgive myself for imagining I was in charge. I am willing to do my part in the Plan for all Happiness throughout time and space.

Because I don't know what my earth plane
part is today, I'll ask by praying.

The training continues, and the Plan moves forward…

My part in The Plan is important, but I am not in *charge* of what it looks like. My part is to listen and follow instructions.

By listening and following instructions, I will find the joy, peace and love of God and extend it. That might have nothing to do with what I thought it was when I first woke up this morning (before I asked). Guilt is an attack thought; it's emotional violence. Gandhi himself said that he was not the perfect master. He was always evolving ... always trying new things to continue his own mind training.

What might Gandhi say to us today? Gandhi, who was always experimenting and trying different techniques, fine tuning and allowing movement, might say, "Martyrdom isn't good for the health. Guilt attacks the mind that holds it." Because we are one, *Really One*, when we increase the belief in guilt in another, we are attacking our *Self*.

"Attack thoughts therefore make you vulnerable in your own mind, which is where the attack thoughts are."
ACIM Workbook Lesson 26

When I notice the temptation to want to make someone feel guilty, I *stop*. My True Self does not want to increase guilt. My Whole Self extends joy, love and peace. Guilt is emotional violence that I have used against myself and try to get rid of by turning on someone else. The temptation to want someone else to feel guilty is the attempt to separate. I must be pushing an agenda, a separate will. That is always coming from ego. It's an opportunity for me to recognize the unloving thought coming up in my mind and give it to Spirit. When I let go of my little plans, it starts to dawn on me that guilt couldn't possibly be real. How could God's Will be done if guilt were real? I'll rest quietly in my seat with that for a while.

Choo ... Choo ... Choo ... Choo ...

We really do need practice. Our minds are very undisciplined. Judgment is an attack on the Self. It has become such a habit that we don't even notice the belief in guilt is in our own minds. Without practice, we actually *believe* our meaningless, separation thoughts. We make them up and convince ourselves that *other* people are causing our unloving thoughts. They *conditioned* us! The *world* made us judge! The *separate* world, people, parents, religion ... some outside force is responsible for my mind. God is Love. I am One with God and everyone. But someone *else made* me think lovelessly. Our own joke doesn't even seem funny. When we decide to stop judging, we stop making excuses and turn to the Mind of Wholeness.

"Every situation properly perceived becomes an opportunity to heal the Son of God."

ACIM.19.1.2

Stop right now and re-read the last sentence.

Read it once more.

"Every situation properly perceived becomes an opportunity to heal the Son of God."

Go find something to write on. I'll wait.

Jot down the sentence this way:

"Every situation interpreted by the Higher Mind becomes an opportunity to heal."

Now write this:

"Every situation is an Enlightenment Opportunity."

Say this out loud. (If you are in public, think it firmly in your heart-mind.)

"Every situation is an Enlightenment Opportunity."

Repeat, "Every situation" a bunch of times.

Put the piece of paper somewhere you will see it every day.

Apply this as if your enlightenment depended on it.

Warning: only do this if you want to live as your Higher Self.

We are so willing to judge the man on the train as bad and Gandhi as better. Someone comes into our lives and throws sand in our face, tells us to get out of the sandbox and go play somewhere else. Okay, it stings for a second. Then what? What is it for?

Sand in the eyes = Enlightenment Opportunity.

When I open my eyes, after blinking the sand out, am I going to see a bully or a savior reminding me of my power to choose to have my mind trained to the light? Here's a divine idea: In the moment of blinking, pray. When I open my eyes, I can choose to behold the Christ, the Light, the Power, Glory, Buddha, Krishna—in You.

Breathing, I can hear the train moving forward.

Choo! Choo! Choo!

I can hear more now.

Choose! Choose! Choose! Choose!

By choosing to acknowledge the light in that person, I am using my Enlightened Mind. I am no longer lying on the tracks in victim posture. I am accessing my Power. My Spiritual Eye is opening. The train is accelerating. We are all on it. Destination: Oneness!

We wake up and realize we were there already; we just dozed off in our seat.

PRAYER:

Spirit of Love,

Guide our Minds. Help us to look beyond the illusion of separation.

Show us the Oneness beyond all appearance.

We want vision.

This is our willingness to experience the One Love that exists in those who have appeared to insult us.

We want to stop attacking those people with *our* minds.

Spirit of Love, help us to sincerely Love.

Lift attack thoughts off of our Minds.

Spirit of Love, we invite You into our perceptions.

We want to Stand Up. Show us the Love in those who appear to have beaten us down, those who appear to have ordered us out.

In this moment, we remember that we rule our minds.

To stand up to the self-imposed oppression of attack thoughts in our own minds, we give our minds to You. We do this more deeply than ever before.

Show us the One Love Force, the Power of God, in us all.

Show us that this is the One Truth. Ignite Truth in our eyes. Open our Spiritual Eye that we might behold our part in the Universal Happiness Plan.

Help us to Trust the Plan that is operating for the Good of all—for the Happiness of all—throughout time and space.

We are willing for the movement of our Mind Training to take us forward.

We are willing to Trust the Perfection already existing now.

You hear the willingness in our hearts.

Thank you for all trainers that exist throughout time and space who have ushered forth Your Perfect Plan.

Give us the vision to recognize that everyone is a trainer, a teacher, a perfect partner in our Awakening to the Truth that We are One.

Thank you.

Amen.

CHANGE YOUR FOCUS

FORGIVING FORGIVENESS

When asked about his spiritual teachers, the Dalai Lama once answered, "Although many brilliant and inspiring teachers have shaped my life, my strongest influence, without a doubt, was Chairman Mao. Because of our opposing views on the future of Tibet, I experienced numerous hardships over a period of many years. Without Mao, I would not have truly learned about forgiveness." (He said this in Tibetan.)

I had a Chairman Mao. My Chairman Mao taught me about forgiveness too. It was apparent to me that My Mao was a guilty dictator. My Mao occupied my mind with thoughts of guilt. During this time, peace fled the landscape of my awareness. I wanted peace (I told myself), but My Mao caused the upset. It was all My Mao's fault! I had better Forgive My Mao.

I tried *really, really* hard to forgive this brutal dictator, plunderer of my peace. Even though My Mao was guilty, I exuded spirituality and innocence. I would demonstrate proper behavior by smiling sweetly, no matter what they did. This bad person might turn into a good person (like me). They would see the heights of my spiritual elevation. Perhaps my innocence would rub off on them. (After all, My

Mao needed it!) But I still felt like yak butter. This approach wasn't working. My Mao refused to change.

Clearly, I needed to take this to a Higher Authority, so I discussed the matter with Marianne Williamson. She advised me to hold a thirty-day prayer vigil. As I was very willing to forgive (change) My Mao, I held the vigil. Every day I prayed for the dirty, rotten scoundrel. I prayed to forgive the guilty, abusive dictator who also had a facial wart and a bad haircut.

For some reason this did not work.

I kept renewing the vigil. Months appeared to pass. I tried with all of my little might. There was no peace in the land. Sensing I needed a new approach, I consulted a Christian friend who suggested fasting. I was willing to try *anything* to recapture my peace. I really wanted to forgive (change) this scoundrel, so I gave up chocolate for a whole month!

(This only lasted for *one* month.)

By seeing My Mao as guilty, I was voluntarily sacrificing my peace. I had blotted peace out of my awareness by believing the grievance story in my head.

> *"The secret of salvation is but this: that you are doing this unto yourself."*
>
> *ACIM 27.IX.83*

Armed with chocolate and determination, I consulted an Indian yogi. His studio was filled with familiar fragrances of tulsi, sandalwood and Nag Champa. The yogi walked on his hands and stood on his head. He spoke of inner light. When I asked him how to forgive My Mao he said, "Stop focusing on the other person and heal yourself." That sounded familiar. It was also relaxing.

I heard about a Forgiveness Conference taking place in Philadelphia and registered immediately. The day arrived and there was a snowstorm but I didn't care. I would Forgive My Mao. That dictator had stolen my peace for long enough! I drove through the snow, got lost, found and finally arrived at the conference. I reminded the Holy Spirit (out loud, in the parking lot) of my great and mighty willingness to forgive. "Behold, I have driven in snow, across state lines!"

Presenters at the conference offered various points of view about forgiveness. Some presenters did not believe in it. *The ideas appeared to conflict.* I drove home to New Jersey going, "Huh?" But the conference packet included a little red forgiveness book. At home, I opened up my little red forgiveness book to a subsection called, "Forgiveness vs. Enabling."

Versus?!

All the clocks in Pink Floyd's song "Time" went off in my head. I read on. It said, "Forgiveness is *not* enabling. *You can be forgiven for stepping in front of a speeding bus, but you will still get run over by the bus.*" You mean I could forgive without stepping in front of the bus? It was *safe* to forgive? It wouldn't kill me? (And I could eat chocolate?)

Suddenly, I was willing to see forgiveness differently.

When we hand a situation over to the Holy Spirit for healing, we are also letting go of the form. If we are trying to

31

hold on to form, we aren't really releasing the situation. The
Holy Spirit hears our hearts and will wait until we are *really*
ready to let go. I had been afraid to forgive because I didn't
know what it meant. The Holy Spirit is our True Protection.
I read the sentence from the red book and let it sink in
a couple of different ways. "Forgiveness does not mean
enabling." "Forgiveness means *not* enabling." Freedom rose
in my heart. My defenses relaxed and my mind flashed on
something *else* Marianne Williamson had told me. She said
this person was a discarded aspect of ... *me*!

It didn't kill me.

When Marianne shared that wisdom, I still secretly
wanted to be separate. But now I wanted to *heal* more than
I wanted to be right. Peace was more important than my
grievance. I let go of *my* conflicting wishes. While focusing
on the person's *behavior,* I had told myself how very *uncouth*
they were to act out the things I *only thought.* "How tacky!"
I judged. It had not occurred to me that the person was
giving me the opportunity to *look* at my error thoughts and
forgive them, allowing them to be undone. My Mao was a
Liberator! A Bodhisattva! This person had come to deliver
me from *my* attack thoughts by acting them out for me. I
could see them and ask the Holy Spirit to heal my mind.

Then I read the *Song of Prayer.*
It only hurt for a minute.

This sweet-sounding Supplement to *A Course in
Miracles* has a whole section called *Forgiveness-to-Destroy.*
This part had no mercy on me. It said *Forgiveness-to-Destroy*

is a *weapon* used to make ourselves feel "better-than" other people! It explained that if we make ourselves into martyrs, we are actually trying to get our innocence at the cost of our brother's guilt. We are trying to separate our brother from God.

"Here must the aim be clearly seen, for this may pass as meekness and as charity instead of cruelty. Is it not kind to be accepting of another's spite, and not respond except with silence and a gentle smile? Behold, how good are you who bear with patience and with saintliness the anger and the hurt another gives, and do not show the bitter pain you feel." (Song of Prayer 2.11)

破获！

(That's Chinese for "busted!")

I do not have to suffer for innocence. (The Son of God cannot suffer and does not want to suffer.) Innocence is not a commodity that I can win in a competition or earn through bargains or behavior. We can't earn it, learn it, gain it or lose it. We can't have more or less of it. Innocence is our True nature. I am already innocent, You are already innocent and so is the Artist Formerly Known as Mao.

If I am "accepting of another's spite" and not setting a healthy boundary at the level of form, I'm trying to prove something. I'm trying to prove guilt (in the name of my "holiness"). Once this ancient Chinese secret came to light, I saw I had been *afraid* to set a boundary. I had put on a show in my head about my spiritual saintliness when I was really just plain kung-foo-chicken.

"Illusions recognized must disappear."
ACIM Workbook Lesson 187

When I mixed up form and content, I withheld my happiness from my awareness. Our True Innocence has nothing to do with form. Now I place my relationships in the Holy Spirit's care. Sometimes form changes. Sometimes I set boundaries at the level of form. That allows peace to reign in the land for all. I still look both ways before I cross the street in China. (Have you *seen* the traffic over there?)

Forgiving Forgiveness has allowed me to remember Who we all are at the level of content and follow the True Leader Within. My True Leader informs my decisions on the level of form while I am here allowing my mind to be healed. To quote the Indian yogi, "Stop focusing on the other person and heal yourself."

PRAYER:

Spirit of Love,

You hear my heart. I am willing to hear it too.

I am willing to be honest about my motives.

Help me recognize that the Truth is safe.

When I am tempted to blame, Guide my focus to the Answer.

Help me remember that You are the Answer God gave me.

Teach me the difference between a boundary and a defense.

Help me identify what an unset boundary feels like.

When I recognize an unset boundary, give me the words so that love speaks through me.

I let go of what I think love will look like.

I place my relationships in Your loving care.

Amen

Practice Following Guidance

Can You Hear Me Meow?

As part of a formal musical education, musicians study ear training. Through practice, we cultivate the skill of identifying pitches, intervals and rhythms by listening. Everyone is born with this natural ability, and we *develop* it through practice. We put in the effort to hone our talents. Babies learn how to identify words in the same manner. Adults work with babies very patiently. "Ma Ma. Da Da. Ma Ma. Da Da." With repetition, the baby gets the idea and learns to associate the sound with other senses. Next, they learn to talk back. Learning how to walk and talk is part of our early childhood education.

Eventually, the baby grows up and learns how to talk to God. The next step is learning how to listen to God. Learning how to listen to God is part of our spiritual education. This part requires repetition, willingness to put in the effort and patience. The Holy Spirit is the Voice for God. As we mature on our spiritual path, we learn how to answer the call God has been imparting through our Divine Communication Link. When we hear Holy Guidance, we are receiving the happy communication from God. Our Creator is always broadcasting. We have to tune in to the Holy Channel to receive the messages.

Some people tell me they can't hear Guidance. But we are always listening to something. In any moment, we are listening to the guidance of the ego (hallucinating), or we are tuning in to the Voice for God. To recognize the Holy Spirit, we have to *want* to listen to the Holy Channel. God gave us the free will to choose love or fear. The answer to all of our apparent problems is: choose the Voice for God. Turn down the volume on the fear channel. Consciously listen to the Voice of Love. When we listen to the Voice of Love, we get the message: All One Love. (Bob Marley listened to the Holy Channel.)

When we try to solve our own problems, the ego is talking to itself. The ego's answers might occasionally sound intelligent, but they never work. If we already recognized the answers to our problems (consciously), we would not believe in them anymore. The ego is not the answer. When we try to "figure out" a problem, we are only chasing our tails.

> *"Perception cannot obey two masters, each asking for messages of different things in different languages. What fear would feed upon, love overlooks. What fear demands, love cannot even see."*
>
> *ACIM 19.V.a*

Several times a day, my dog stares at me intently. She tilts back her head and barks, "Woof! Woof! Woof!" If I don't feel like going outside, I can pretend I don't understand what, "Woof (Take)! Woof (Me)! Woof (Out)!" means. I can use my free will to play dumb and stall. If we use our free will to avoid Holy Guidance, we are using a delay tactic. More will be revealed. When I play dumb with my dog, she barks, *"Woof (Right)!! Woof (Now)!!"* Then I can use my free will to either take her for a walk or continue to delay. If I continue to delay, my dog will send the message in another form. She makes sure the message is unmistakable.

The ego likes to say, "Obviously God is wrong." It also pretends, "I do not understand what God is trying to communicate; I am so dumb." Only our willingness is necessary to receive Holy Guidance. It is the Will of the Divine that we communicate. Our will is not separate. When we are dedicating our day to receiving Holy Guidance, we recognize the difference between the voice of fear and the Voice of Love. We recognize the objections as nonsense. The strength of God goes with us as we carry out the instructions from our True Inner Teacher. Don't expect the ego to approve the messages of The Holy Spirit. As we let go of valuing the ego's voice, Holy Guidance rises into our awareness.

The Holy Spirit is in every mind. To tune in to Holy Guidance, we must listen for the love in everyone. Someone might tell us a story about their ski trip and words will stand out from their story that have nothing to do with skiing. The Holy Spirit will use their vacation story to send us a message. Sometimes we hear Very Clear Thoughts in our own heads. We might see images in meditation or in a dream. Perhaps we will receive an inner prompt to go somewhere or not go. The physical world offers messages too. A song will play on the radio with lyrics that speak directly into our heart. Someone could hand us just the right book. The Holy Spirit is a Multi-Medium. With practice, we become adept at recognizing these communications.

We practice listening for the Voice of God in others. By setting this intention, we are choosing to remember the holiness of everyone. By our decision to communicate on the level of holiness, we are recalling the Truth. We can make this Divine Decision at any moment. Someone can be yelling at us, or we can be melting down. We can stop and remember everyone is a Holy Son of God. In the moments of temptation, we *re-call* the Holy Spirit into our minds. "Earth to Holy Spirit—Come in Holy Spirit!" (Do this silently.) The Holy Spirit answers every call. Suddenly, we will interpret the situation differently, or the other person will yell something entirely out of context. (It's really funny when that happens. Hearing the Holy Spirit yell something is hilarious.)

> *"The message your brother gives you is up to you. What does he say to you? What would you have him say? Your decision about him determines the message you receive. Remember that the Holy Spirit is in him, and His Voice speaks to you through him."*
>
> *ACIM 8.11.111*

Whenever I am on my way to meet someone, I say a prayer. "Let this be a holy encounter. Let only the Holy Spirit speak and hear through both/all of us." By setting this intention in advance, I am inviting the Love into the situation. This dedicates the situation to the Holy Spirit's purpose. Remember—God has a Plan for Salvation and so does the ego. Each of us plays as an essential part in God's Plan. God communicates to us about our part in the Divine Plan through Holy Guidance. (Some call it intuition.)

Only God's Plan will work. I am so thankful the ego's plans won't work. The ego is the belief in separation and has lots of separate plans. *The Course* calls the ego's plans "self-initiated plans." As we unlearn our identification with the ego, we let go of listening to its delusional plans. The ego's separate plans are all-about-me. Even if the ego's plans seem to be about others, they are building up the little ego's belief in itself. Because we cannot see how The Universal Happiness Plan fits together, we can't direct the Plan. We don't know what's going on throughout time and space. Workbook Lesson 135 of *The Course* reminds us, *"A healed mind does not plan. It carries out the plans which it receives through listening to Wisdom that is not its own. It waits until it has been taught what should be done and then proceeds to do it."*

By listening to divine wisdom, we receive our assignments as instruments of The Universal Happiness Plan. We don't have to know how everyone's part works together. We are only responsible for our part. Our journey has been individually designed for the healing of our mind. As the blocks to love are removed from our awareness, the whole is uplifted.

> *"The curriculum is highly individualized. And all aspects are under the Holy Spirit's particular care and guidance. Ask and He will answer." Manual for Teachers 29.2*

There is a branch in the road at which we can't continue believing in our own little plans. We have come too far to continue listening to the ego. We stand at the juncture because of the progress already made. Our faith has shifted. We can stand at the place in time and pretend we don't know which way to go. But Holy Guidance *is* in our minds. Now we are choosing between Holy Guidance and delay.

At this point, we have learned that we want to follow God's Plan. Our resistance to God's Will has wavered. We are God's Will. God's Will is: joy, love and peace. By following the Plan that has been perfectly constructed for us, we find out What We Really Are. So far, my learning has gone like this:

1. Became honest I was afraid of God's Will. (Not HS's fault.)
2. Admitted that only God's Plan works.
3. Turned to only wanting God's Will no matter what. (Enthusiastic devotion!)
4. Noticed that other people's ego plans for me never work.
5. Realized I have to check within before saying "yes" to other people's plans for me no matter how fun they sound.
6. Repeat steps #2 and #3.

Each step has been a matter of practice, just like ear training. The more I train my ear to listen to the Voice of Love, the better I can hear the higher frequencies. (Dogs know this.) When I'm not listening to the love in others, I can't play in tune with them. Sometimes I have to listen *past* the static. I have to adjust my ears and really concentrate. I have to find their higher frequency. Tuning in is a skill. It becomes easier with experience. The process is kind. We learn one step at a time.

One day, I wrote "Thy Will Be Done" on my whiteboard. My body started to tremble. I erased it and wrote something else. When I recognized the utter futility of my "own" plans, I was ready to commit to God's Will. Eventually, I was ready to take the next step. I became a highly motivated candidate for God's Will. When I realized that other people's little will for me didn't work, I dumped their self-initiated plans easily. The ego did not like this one bit, as I was no longer a sucker for shiny objects, flattery or promises of instant fame. God's Universal Happiness Plan works. Other plans won't. That used to tick me off. Now it makes me incredibly happy. (See? It works!)

7. Forgive myself and others for listening to the ego's plan.

Here we go again with forgiveness. When I notice other people's ego plans for me, I have the opportunity to forgive myself for my past self-initiated plans. Thank you Self-Forgiveness Opportunity Delivery People!

8. Keep Practicing. Keep forgiving. Keep up the Good Work.

We are all in training. Jesus learned to hear only One Voice. *A Course in Miracles* says it was the final lesson he learned, and we are all equal in our ability to learn. When we see ourselves or others as guilty for listening to the ego, we are listening to the ego. We can choose forgiveness. We can learn a lot from babies. They have great dedication to learning. When they fall down, they get up again. With practice, their recovery time quickens. They trust they can do it. Babies trust the process. After they learn how to crawl, they concentrate on walking. The next thing you know it, they remember they can dance.

Making Difficult Decisions

Recently, I noticed numerous people talking about *making difficult decisions*. At first, I had a thought, *"Oh no, am I going to have to make a difficult decision?"* But then I realized, *that* was a fear thought. I remembered there *are* no difficult decisions. We are always making the same decision—am I going to follow the voice for fear or the Voice of Love?

Can *that* be a difficult decision?

God is good all the time. *Which voice will I follow?* Any time it seems as if I am making a decision, I am actually following the guidance of fear or the Guidance of Love. Fear is a liar. The choice is easy if I want to be happy. I can form a healthy habit of giving my life to God *decision by decision.* At all times we are listening to either love or fear, so decisions are continuous. Who am I choosing *with*—love or fear? Am I listening to the Holy Spirit, or am I listening to fear thoughts? Where am I placing my trust?

Trust is identification.

It helps me to start out first thing in the morning, as soon as I wake up, to remember that what I *really* want is what God Wills for me. I align to the day that God has for me. In this way, I am dedicating the day in *advance* to Love.

PRACTICE:

God's Will for me is joy.

God's Will for me is love.

God's Will for me is peace.

Our Will is the same.

I can have a day of joy, love and peace if I let the Holy Spirit be in charge of all my decisions…

I will let the Holy Spirit *interpret* all situations as they unfold. How I interpret each situation is a decision. It is a decision to listen to love or fear.

I give my willingness to let the day be interpreted by the One Who knows Who I Am; the One Who knows that God is my Source…

I align to the highest use of me…

Amen

When I ask for Guidance, sometimes I will hear something or see something in meditation. Lots of times I do not. By giving the offering of willingness each morning, the Guidance comes throughout the day. It comes in different ways, in ways I understand and can receive. It's important to remember the part about letting the Holy Spirit interpret the situations that unfold. If I judge a situation, *that* is a decision to listen to the voice of fear. God does not condemn. Perhaps my schedule will get shuffled around. I can remember, "I can't see the Whole Plan." My *life circumstances* might get shuffled around. I can either judge or remember, "My life is being re-aligned for the highest use of me."

There is no order of difficulty in Truth.

By giving my willingness in the morning, I am deciding to go into the day remembering that my *purpose* is the peace, love and joy of God. This way I am *not* going into the day with ego/fear agendas. By starting the day with the purpose of the peace, love and joy of God, I am extending this into all of my encounters and situations. Throughout the day, I pause and tune in, asking for the loving interpretation. I remember why I am *choosing* the loving interpretation. By remembering my purpose, I protect my mind from placing ego demands. Through practice, I learn to remember I already have everything I really want. I can decide for God every day. We all have that Voice for God within us. It's our integrity. Turning away from it and following the voice of fear is the basic cause of guilt. Our emotions tell us when we have chosen fearfully. Through spiritual practice, we can align to the joy within. Everyone can do it, because it's within all of us.

Sometimes we have already judged. We decided in advance that there was only one way to see a situation. (Or maybe multiple choices: *"anything but that God!"*) Our mind is not open to hearing the loving interpretation because we're trying to control. Our attachment to the world looking a certain way is causing us to forget that God is our Source. Our focus on outcome is blocking our awareness of the joy, love and peace of God. We have forgotten Who We Are. We're not feeling ourSelf. Did you ever say that? "I'm not feeling mySelf today."

I had a situation in which I was in such resistance, such fear. And then I realized that the *only* problem was that the situation was not serving the ego. That was it. That was the *only* problem. I am not an ego. God created me. There *was* no problem. The situation didn't change. I stopped listening to the condemning voice. The fear left. The situation was not serving the ego; it was serving the Christ. The ego shut up and ran away. There seemed to be a problem because I had forgotten my one decision is to let the Holy Spirit decide for me. I had forgotten to ask the Holy Spirit. But then I remembered, because I did not like the way I *felt!*

No matter what the ego is screaming, we can remember that we can choose again. Fear is *not* Who We Are! We are God's Happiness. That's why God's Will and Our Will are the Same. I can remember I really want to experience my Oneness with God. Our Will is One. Our Self is One. I am an expression of the Love of God, the Joy of God. You are an expression of the Love of God, the Joy of God.

Think of someone you love. With your mind, tell them, "You are an expression of the Love and Joy of God." Now call to mind someone you are tempted not to love. (Yes, *them.*) With your mind, tell them, "You are an expression of the Love and Joy of God." Now tell yourself, "I am an expression of the Love and Joy of God." It takes practice to remember the Truth consistently...consistent spiritual practice. To be unconditionally happy, I must ask the Holy Spirit to teach me what I *really* want.

We find the Love of God within us by valuing It. When I am judging/condemning a situation, I am forgetting to let the Holy Spirit interpret it for me. The situation has been perfectly planned for me. Judgment is not coming from the Voice of God. It is not coming from my Source. Judgment is self-deception. I can't hear the Holy Spirit when I am judging.

When I was younger in my journey, I heard "don't judge." We have all heard that. But I didn't understand *how* not to judge or *why* not to judge. I didn't yet understand that judgment was self-deception. It's a decision to listen to the voice of fear. I had not yet learned to ask the Holy Spirit to *decide for me*, I had no discernment. Discernment is following the Holy Spirit in decision making. I wanted *my* way in the world. I did not perceive my own best interests. Sometimes I really *knew* the answer (in my gut) but didn't ask because I wanted what I thought I wanted in the world. So I decided *not* to ask. And those situations never worked out the way I expected them to work out, anyway. I couldn't hide things from the Holy Spirit, call it "non-judgment," and then try to force a solution. That was *not* non-judgment; it was denial.

I learned that I *wanted discernment*; that I really wanted the Holy Spirit's Guidance. I learned which Voice to Trust. *A Course in Miracles* tells me exactly what to do to lay aside all judgment. Here it is—I must *"ask only that I be taught what I really want in every circumstance"* (M.4.9). I have to be taught what I really want by the aspect of my mind who recognizes Who I Really Am. The Holy Spirit is not making anything more important than the Truth. The Holy Spirit values the Christ in me.

The Holy Spirit values the Christ in You.

Remember this.

Say it out loud:

The Holy Spirit values the Christ in me.

Say it again!

*The Holy Spirit **Loves** the Christ in me.*

This is the Guide for me—the Guide that recognizes the Christ in me. I am no longer interested in the advice of anyone coming from fear or guilt. Fear's advice no longer compels me. Divine Love sees me as an Expression of God, and is available to Guide me. That is the advice I am interested in following. The voice of fear will tell us what we imagine we need. Fear will tell us its *conditions.* "Here are my conditions for being happy; for being lovable, for loving. If those conditions change or do not change, I will not be happy or lovable and will attempt to make other people unhappy too. Someone will be guilty if I don't get my way." That's the voice for fear and we can tell by our emotions.

When we sense the fear, we can stop. WE CAN STOP. Notice "this is fear." The ego is screaming what it demands. It always wants something that will not last forever. It's a setup for guilt, for loss of peace. *A Course in Miracles* teaches us, *"Perhaps it is not yet quite clear to you that each decision that you make is one between a grievance and a miracle."* That makes sense, and it motivates me to ask the Holy Spirit to Guide me about everything.

To let a decision be Guided by the Holy Spirit—that's a miracle! Let's not take it for granted. We can be Guided by the Holy Spirit—a Spirit that's Holy and recognizes the Christ in us! Divine Love will guide us through our day, through our life, and all *we* have to do is give our willingness. How beautiful is that?! The other choice is to ignore our integrity and decide under the advisement of fear, which is the basic cause of guilt. What does guilt do? It projects. There is the grievance choice. So by our conscious decision to let Divine Love be our Guide, we are choosing to bring the peace, love and joy of God to everyone we will encounter throughout the day, and to everyone we will even *think* about.

Wow!

We don't even need to know how to do this. There's nothing fancy involved. We are welcoming the Wisdom that already dwells within us. The Holy Spirit can't fail. *It's the Holy Spirit.* By forming the healthy habit of dedicating each day to the leadership of love, peace and joy, we become increasingly willing to stay in alignment. When we make a mistake, we turn back to love quickly because the contrast is obvious. We no longer want to serve the voice for fear because it doesn't feel good. We are learning not to identify with it.

Through spiritual practice, we recognize that we value joy, love and peace. The *"I'm right"* voice offers nothing but pain. Miracles become a conscious priority. With practice, we recognize each decision is the same decision, and it's an easy one. We are listening to either the voice for grievances or the voice for miracles. Every form of distress is unforgiveness.

God never wills for our distress.

Our Christ Mind is not holding a grievance.

When I am distressed in *any* way, I can recognize that I have let the ego decide what something means. I have let fear interpret for me. The Holy Spirit knows Who We Really ARE. By practicing asking the Holy Spirit to decide for me, interpret for me, I am learning to *doubt the ego* instead of doubting God's Plan for my life. Now, when the ego has a great big fit, I quickly recognize that if the ego is *sooooo threatened*, the Christ Self is being *Blessed!* Whatever is happening must be the highest and best for Christ, which includes all of Creation. Christ is The Self that God knows...the One Self. I TRUST GOD!

I am not here to serve the ego. I *am* here for Divine Love. The light of Christ must be shining brightly for the ego to be "melting." I therefore love this situation just the way it is. God knows Who I Am. I choose to agree with God. It's the wise choice, the discerning decision. I make this one decision and repeat as needed. The rewards of peace, love and joy keep reinforcing the choice. Who I Really Am is what I really want—the Self that God Created. So I follow the One Who already knows me, just the way God created me.

All I have to do is ask.

RELEASE PHANTOM PAIN

WHAT ARE YOU TRYING TO PROVE?

In one week, I came upon three, three-legged dogs. The family of the first three-legged dog explained that this dear canine sometimes experiences phantom pain. Like human amputees, this dog sometimes experiences pain in the missing leg. Two more three-legged dogs came along with a message. "All pain is phantom pain." When we are upset, we are reacting to what is no longer there. We are seeing the past.

All pain is phantom pain.
Woof.

Many years ago, a *four*-legged dog attacked my friend Bette. "Vicious Childhood Dog" travels around in Bette's upper subconscious mind as a spot of unforgiveness. She carries the memory of "Vicious Childhood Dog" with her into every encounter with a canine. In her mind, *every* dog is dangerous. The canine from her childhood is a "shadow figure."

Bette has been an important person in my life for decades. She has come to my house only once. She did not enjoy the visit. When she came to my home, she could not perceive the friendly Cocker Spaniel sporting a pink bow.

Bette saw DANGER and refused to come back. My friend has even compared my dog to a serial killer.

My friend sees only the past. She is not seeing what is right in front of her. Her mind is playing tricks on her. Her mind is pulling her own leg. Bette's perception of my dog teaches *me*. Bette's pet trick is a reminder to me. When *I* am upset, *I* am reliving the past. Each moment is a real-time opportunity to hand all loveless, fearful perceptions over for healing. The Holy Spirit knows we are safe already. Our True Self is harmless. Our True Self is incapable of harming or being harmed. God has saved Our True Self forever from all of our ruses. When we are finished with the games, we accept our True Self and enjoy life. We hand over the unforgiving perceptions. Then we relax and take a nap. (All dogs and cats know this. Even squirrels know it.)

The mind uses everything for the purposes of love or for the purposes of fear. Thoughts are loving or unloving. This also applies to time. Time itself is really nothing but an idea. We have given it meaning. We are completely convinced that we are living in linear time. Do we *want* to continue to experience the ego's use of time? If we would rather use time in the service of God, we must train our minds to stay (in the present).

Love the dog you're with.

The ego uses time to defend fear, calling endless witnesses to prove that guilt is real. But guilt is a delay tactic. Part of our mind knows it's lying. The mind made a character for itself and for everyone else. It has assigned roles. Where *is* guilt anyway? *What* is it? Guilt is an idea that we made up in the past and decided to keep. We wrote it to support the fictional drama of our stories. The "bad guys" *need* guilt to carry out the roles we assigned to them. As long as "bad guys" are being bad, the "hero" can use them to make himself "good" by comparison.

We look for conflict by seeking evidence to support our cliff-hanging tension. We regurgitate old plot lines, anything to keep the old pain alive. Obviously, "bad guys" caused all the drama, (not us). We must be "innocent," right God? It must be someone *else* who caused my belief in guilt.

Are we tuning in to the Thoughts of God?

In any area of your life in which you are not consistently happy, ask yourself:

- What am I trying to prove?

- What do I really want?

- Do I want guilt *or* do I want the peace of God?

"The ego's voice is an hallucination. You cannot expect it to say, 'I am not real.'"

ACIM 8.1.3

The choice for happiness is the decision to notice the difference between reality and fiction. The Truth is obvious when we want it. By being deeply honest, we let go of trying to prove that fiction (separation) is real. We *observe* the ego's attraction to guilt and let it go. The Truth in our Mind wants our healing, literally *wills* it. We have the power to choose. What do we want to see? Who do we want to be? *What we want to believe about others is what we want to believe about ourselves.*

We think we are afraid because something outside *happened* and *proved* we are not safe. But the outside world reflects our decision, showing us which master our mind is serving. *We use outer conditions to prove who we are.* The ego screams, "They went first! That dog bit me! Here is the evidence that I am not safe. Therefore I am vulnerable." (The ego convinces us of this while we are sitting on the couch drinking raspberry iced tea.) But the world did not come first; it's a spin-off. When we *want* the Truth, we let go of valuing our past interpretations. When we want the peace of God, we turn within. The characters in our dream come along and act out our beliefs so we can observe them. These characters offer the opportunity to recognize our unhealed thoughts. Everyone gives us the opportunity to choose happiness instead of fear.

All unforgiveness is a distraction from remembering, "I am as God created me." In any moment, we can let go of the meaning we have given to our past thoughts by giving them to the Loving Changeless Mind. The Loving Mind is the "I" that God created. The Loving Mind is in everyone.

"We am as God created we" is not good English. Even my dog knows that. (She is an English Cocker Spaniel.) The "I" that God created is all of us. As we let go of our resistance to love, we are released from our past choices for fear. By letting go of what is not real, everything unlike love is dissolved. Our lives are prepared for a different future. We are cleared for take-off and go forward attracting love because love is in our minds. When we ask God how we can perceive a person or situation without judgment, we enter the miraculous state. We have laid aside our insistence on being right and chosen *Our Right Mind.*

When we judge, we are holding on to illusion. We are choosing the problem by denying the Whole Mind. Whenever we feel the peace of a relationship or situation being threatened (and we know when we are losing the loving feeling), we can stop and instantly offer the situation, the relationship, to love. It *is* simple. We don't have to know what to do. The part of our mind that is eternally connected to God knows.

As we get out of the way, the meaningless thoughts that conspired to create whatever happened are no longer present. They pass because of our *willingness.* Our minds move forward and into the presence of God's Love.

We have made space for Truth.
God's Will is done.

We welcome the answer the instant we relinquish our delay tactics. Miracles exist outside of the time-space continuum (that's why we call them miracles). The ego mind cannot perform them. Miracles are divine interventions of love—corrective measures that return the mind to its natural loving state.

"To heal is to make happy."
ACIM 5.1.1

My ex-exterminator taught me the joy of laying my judgment to rest. My ex-exterminator used to bug me. I formed opinions about the way he did business and was sure those opinions were right. My opinions (judgments) about my ex-exterminator blocked love and happiness (Truth) from my awareness. My ex-exterminator had opinions too. We had a contract, so he was part of my life on an ongoing basis. One day, I decided I wanted the Love of God more than my ideas about an exterminator. I decided to let go of my judgments and experience the love. When that brother showed up at my door, I would *love* him! I *resolved* to experience our Oneness! Our different ideas no longer mattered to me. Those little differences were *nothing*. The Truth of our Oneness, our love as brother and sister in God was *everything*! While awaiting my Now Beloved Brother, the clock ticked. Love beamed from my heart to this bug-exterminating brother.

Tick, Tock, Tick.

Tick. Tick. Tick.

Tick.

I surrounded My Brother with the Light of God.

We are One!

Tick. Tick. Tick.

The dog wanted a walk. I decided to call the company and find out when My Beloved Brother would arrive, as the appointment had long since passed. The company informed me that my contracts were null and void. Yeah! Free at Last! My heart leapt with joy. Our assignment was complete. On the surface, it seemed as if our relationship had been about getting rid of bugs. Really, my learning assignment was to remember to love. Nothing can bug me but *my* thoughts. When I decided to *love* my exterminator, our mission was complete. We weren't a compatible long-term relationship. We were of One Mind about this. But I had to remember to love my Brother before the job was complete. Our only *real* job is to remember to love. God Bless You, Ex-Exterminator!

> *"There are no small upsets. They are all equally disturbing to my peace of mind."*
>
> ACIM Workbook Lesson 6

When pain (*or even mild irritation*) comes up into our conscious awareness, we can give our perceptions to the Spirit of Love to be corrected. Something has arisen from the upper subconscious for release. Our projections show us *our* hidden thoughts and fears. We are imagining *that which God did not create.* If it's not love, it's fear. These are *the thoughts **we*** have given meaning and hidden away from sight.

Every Child of God knows this:
She who smelt it, dealt it.

We know about the law of attraction. Our *hidden* thoughts also attract. Our phantom pains bring our subconscious wounds, our unhealed thoughts to the surface for healing. If we push them back down, pretend we don't smell them or feel them (lie), blame the dog, *we are choosing to keep them.* We will have another opportunity for release. They have come ... to go.

(This too shall pass.)
It is safe to let go.
SPIRIT IS BEHIND EVERYTHING.

We are the light of the world. On the *conscious* level, we look
like separate bodies. When we count on our physical senses to
perceive for us, we will believe that we are bodies. The physical
(conscious) level shows us the belief in separation, the dimension where there could be attack and darkness. It seems real.
It appears to be solid. But we are perceiving projected images
of our thoughts. *A Course in Miracles* interchanges "physical
eye" with the word "ego." "Spiritual Eye" is synonymous with
"Holy Spirit," "Spirit of Love," and others. (This Spirit has
aliases.) Our physical eyes look at a body and see separation.
The conscious level is the realm of perceptual distortion. *The
Course* reminds us that perception is not knowledge.

By letting the Holy Spirit see for us, we can see that all
life literally shines, emits light at a level the physical eyes
cannot see. Our naked eyes don't see it (even when we're
naked). The light rises into our awareness as we become
willing to Trust its presence in our brother. The blessing
that we extend, we receive. Our willingness to look beyond
the physical and give faith to the light activates our memory
of God. By our willingness to Trust beyond the surface perception, we give our mind to Spirit. This is the choice to
value light more than what our outer eyes are showing us.

Light cannot be fractured. The sun shines and reflects
on bays, oceans, ponds and puddles. It's the same sun. The
sun is a symbol in our dream. When we allow Spirit to lead
our minds, the symbols of the dream are interpreted lovingly.
Then we radiate love naturally. Our bodies become communication devices for love. We reflect love, light in the dream.

Our hidden subconscious fears; our dark, icky Wounds-of-Christmas-Past are tucked away in the *upper* subconscious. We are accustomed to thinking of upper as better, but this is just the meaning that we have given to "upper." Think of the upper subconscious as the level just beneath the surface. Have you ever wondered what happens to thoughts and feelings that we deny? What we push down goes into the *upper* subconscious. (Hate? *Who, me?*) The *upper* subconscious stores our hidden thoughts and phantom pains.

Where is the light?

We must look further beneath the surface, past the upper subconscious. The haul is in the depths. We give our willingness to go deeper. Go within! Our *lower (deepest)* subconscious is LIGHT. This is the level of Reality—the Real Will. Our joined mind is the Christ Light.

Stick Figure 1

Happiness is our Universal Will.

The LIGHT, shared Christ Mind wills our Joy. It pushes our hidden, meaningless fears up into our awareness because:

Healing is necessary.
We can handle it.

Stick Figure 2

It's time to give up our meaningless thoughts (unforgiveness).
Phantom pains are the blocks in awareness that cover our shared
light. We need to let them go…Your Joy is essential to the Joy
of the whole. The Son needs you to shine unencumbered.

Aha!

Stick Figure 3

All of our fearful thoughts are variations on a theme—
the belief in separation (unforgiveness). Without our *belief*
that we separated from God, we would have no fear.

"In truth there is nothing to fear. It is very easy to recognize this. But it is very difficult to recognize for those who want illusions to be true."

ACIM Workbook Lesson 48

When we decide that we no longer want to prove that guilt is real, we have become willing. Knowledge is restored from the bottom up. The blocks to love in our mind will rise into conscious awareness. As these dead thoughts surface it is important to remember that they have *come* to *go*. They have come up so we can learn they are nothing. God did not make them, so they are not real. They are meaningless (phantom) thoughts that can be undone. When we hand them over, the Light returns us to our natural state. Light "heals" by establishing the non-existence of darkness. Call the Light by any name that works for you.

There are fancy brain (subcortical activity) studies that deconstruct the science of the "Aha!" moment. I prefer Stick Figures 1, 2 and 3. At the Level of Stick Figure 2, I can ask Spirit, "How can I see My Mao differently?" Then I wait. Sooner or later (usually sooner), I will hear a song, open a book or have a flash of insight. My Mao will transform into my Savior before my eyes. My mind has been returned to its Natural State (Stick Figure 3). All I had to do was ask.

PRACTICE:

Pick a meaningless thought, any meaningless thought. You know which one is ready to go. It has already flashed across the screen of your inner awareness.

God did not create_____.
(Examples: lack, dog bites, betrayal, jealousy, rejection, vulnerability, unworthiness, greed, etc.)

This meaningless thought has come into your conscious awareness for release. It has *come* to *go.*

God *did not* create it. (I am completely serious about this. God did not create it.)

In this moment, we call upon the Divine Mind that is eternally joined with God.

Ask the Spirit of Love (or other alias) to lift this meaningless thought from your precious, perfectly created mind.

Give your consent.

You are shifting your Faith *away* from your meaningless thought now.

By the power of your God-Created Mind, you are giving your Faith *to* the Spirit of Love.

Shifts are Miracles.

The Spirit of Love is on the job now.

All consequences of your previous thought are being undone for you now throughout time and space.

You have invited healing into your mind.

There is no need to try or struggle or do anything.

You are not in charge of the correction. Just sit there.

Relax. You can even hang your head off the couch. I hear it's quite soothing.

There will be a shift in your mind.

The shift might show up immediately.

The healing thought might flash into your awareness later in the day or in a few days.

A highly symbolic dream might give you the gift of insight.

Maybe the same old situation will happen and you will *see it* completely differently.

You will recognize the healing when it comes.

The release *is* underway. Relax, *breathe deeply* and be glad.

Trust.

Amen.

> *"There is no problem in any situation that faith will not solve."*
>
> *ACIM Chapter 17.VIII.65*

LET GO OF YOUR SELF-CONCEPT

Even though Stick Figure 3 looks like the sun, Heaven has nothing to do with the sky. Heaven is the state of no separation. When I ate the Heavenly samosa and was lifted out of time and space, my body was still sitting in a chair at an Indian restaurant. My body might even have been making a funny face. I was not aware of the physical realm. The entirety of my experience was infinite, eternal love. There were people at the table in the restaurant. No one mentioned that my body disappeared, so I assume it was still sitting there.

The world is not reflecting Heaven ... yet (though there *is* proof). *The world is a picture of an inward condition.* Our secret wish for separation shows us a world with problems. We project the conviction called "guilt" onto one another. *(It's his/her/their fault!)* Obviously, someone *else* had the insane idea to separate. *They* caused wars, diseases and economic crises. *We* are the good people who want only world peace, prosperity and eternal Beatles music. (Cue sitar.)

But the world is a picture of *our* state of mind. We can see our hidden thoughts. They aren't really hidden. Our fearful illusions show up as form on this earth. Anything not showing a joyous, loving expression is a hellish thought-form that must be *trans*formed. As we allow our thoughts to be corrected, the earth reflects loving conditions.

"My thoughts are images which I have made."
ACIM Workbook Lesson 15

The ego will tell us we are very innocent, spiritual and good people living in a mean, scary, bad world. If only the *other* people, the bad people would change, the world would be a safe place to live. This is a concept we have made. It is not the Truth because God did not Think it. Concepts are images. Comparative innocence is a bargain made with guilt. It is a self-concept. We are seeing images of others; images of a world, images of a self.

"Your concept of the world depends upon this concept of the self."
ACIM 31.V.53

This mental picture is a replacement we have made for the Truth. It blocks our experience of the Self that God created. The comparatively innocent self is an appearance. We value keeping up this valueless appearance. The appearance is an ego defense. Our Real Innocence is not a consequence of someone else's guilt.

Any self-concept of innocence is a cover-up. Cover stories feature good guys and bad guys that displace thoughts of guilt. *"Someone must fix those guilty people OUT THERE who make the world a scary and bad place!"* We project images of guilt to try to get rid of our untrue ideas about ourselves. The True Self is not an image made by us. Our True Self is a Thought of God.

"Good guy/bad guy" stories show us *semblances* of innocence (not True Innocence) and projections of imagined guilt. Dark images block the vision of our True Innocent Self.

Judgment is an image of innocence being purchased at the expense of our brother's guilt. (They are bad. Therefore, I am good. They are even slightly irritating. Therefore, I am better and good.) This split is the illusion in separate interests. The ego will take any disguise to perpetuate the belief in separation. Judgment is an attack on our own innocence. Judgment is a false perception, a visual misperception. It is impossible because it would require us to be aware of everything that has happened everywhere in the world, everything happening now and everything that will ever happen. The "self-concept" of innocence in which we see ourselves as innocent victims in a bad world peopled by evildoers is an illusion. We are justifying attack thoughts and calling it innocence.

We confuse anger and innocence, hate and love. A self-concept of innocence that has been purchased at the expense of another's guilt is an illusion we have invented and given meaning. But it has no meaning. A self-concept that has no meaning is constantly trying to *find* meaning, constantly trying to attach itself to something to justify its existence. The ego wants to replace our True Identity

(Eternal Innocence). It tries to make a substitute reality. This false image of a self tells us:

"I am ___A___ in the world; therefore, I am good."
"I have ___B___ in the world; therefore, I am good."
"My body ___C___; therefore, I am good."
"I do ___D___ in the world; therefore, I am good."

Our True Will is to be Happy. The part of our Mind that is eternally connected to God knows Itself as our authentic goodness. A, B, C, and D will not last. A, B, C, and D are not what make us good. In fact, A, B, C, and D are images we have made to substitute for Real Innocence. We have this crazy hypothesis, a lie told to ourselves many times. This lie says, "If A (or B or C or D), then I am." The ego thought system rests on the upside-down notion that our existence depends on external, ephemeral conditions. This gives rise to an undercurrent of fear. We have invented images and use them as replacements for our perfectly created Eternal Selves. A, B, C, or D falls away and the lying part of the mind has a fit! As soon as we give our willingness to stop listening to the fit, we notice that without being A in the world, having B in the world, our body being C in the world, or doing D in the world... I Am! It seemed as if we would die when those things fell away, but we didn't. The *image* of ourself as little, separate, and weak did. We find out we aren't the images we made. We are extensions of God.

God is not an image.
God is the experience of Love.
Love is Eternal.

"The Kingdom of Heaven is you."
ACIM 4.IV.41

The minister of my family's Methodist church bravely called the children up to address the congregation every Sunday. My little brother Chris always had something to share. He reported on what was happening in our home. He spoke with no judgment; just a factual account of what he had seen and heard at home. "My Mommy said our dentist charges too much." He kept us on our toes. Before saying or doing anything, we considered whether we wanted it announced to the congregation.

Judgment isn't natural. Little children accept their innocence. Innocence is our natural state. Little children accept they don't know everything. Their innocence makes them happy! They dance as if no one is looking and will invite you to watch. Little children remember they deserve love. When we doubt that we deserve love, we are missing the joy and peace available in every moment. When we judge, we are seeing something that isn't there. Unreal images are blocking the experience of love's presence.

The only way to judge ourselves, others, or situations is by imagining we know everything. When we judge, we're pretending. In any moment, we can remember how much we can't see. Little children trust the Invisible. They even have invisible friends! Little children accept that their plans for the future might change. They're not overly attached. They don't have a long past to drag into the future. Their future is wide open. People used to ask my little brother Chris what he wanted to be when he grew up. For a while he said, "Either a cop or an alligator." He eventually changed his mind. Plans change. Little children have fun in the moment. They don't worry about the future. Worry is unnatural.

When we go through times of change, we can remember what we understood instinctively as children. Our plans might change because we grow up. Our lives reflect our growth. The outside shows us what is going on inside our minds. We don't learn everything all at once. There is more to learn. God is within us all along the way. (We are within God too!) Love never leaves. When we are tempted to worry, we can turn our minds back to what never changes. The Unconditional Innocence that God Created makes us want to dance again. Innocence was the original children's message. When we make up a story about what has to happen, we are defending against the experience of our True Self by clinging to a concept.

Intellectually, we agree that God is Love and God does not judge. To experience what we believe intellectually, we must put our faith into practice. Every situation is an opportunity to experience our Oneness with God. We don't even have to do anything. All we have to do for this spiritual practice is *not* do something—*not* pretend. We can stop pretending we know something. When we are judging, we are pretending. Children are wise. When children pretend, they don't pretend they aren't pretending. They *admit* they're pretending.

> *"Certain it is that all distress does not appear to be but unforgiveness. Yet that is the content underneath the form."*
> *ACIM Workbook Lesson 193*

If we aren't happy, we are pretending to be smarter than God. God's Will for us is happiness. This is not about pushing emotions down but admitting that when we are not in touch with joy, we are judging. But, we can make another choice. The more we practice admitting we have something to learn, the happier we are. So when we forget and judge, we notice right away. Pretending to be aware of everything that has ever happened, is happening now, and will ever happen, doesn't feel good. There is more going on than meets the eye. Eventually, the temptation to tell ourselves another way of seeing the situation subsides. We give ourselves permission to learn from the Spirit of Wholeness Itself. When we release our made-up concepts, we leave space for Truth to shine into our awareness.

The original children's message was about humility. Children hear the inner music. They're practical. Dance now. You are lovable and free. God loves you. Children understand the simplicity of enlightenment. Eat when you're hungry. Sleep when you're tired. If you're full of energy, why take a nap? When you're tired, sleep right where you are. When my brother Brook was a child, he used to lie down on the sidewalk and take a nap in the sun. He didn't judge himself. Dogs and cats do it. The sidewalk is warm. It feels great! Sing when the song is in your heart. Tell the truth because there isn't anything else. Little kids are wise. They accept there is a lot to learn, and that doesn't bother them. They understand they'll learn as they go along. Their hearts and minds are open.

When we learn what little kids comprehend naturally, *we* are becoming wise. We aren't trying to teach ourselves what we don't understand. We let ourselves sing and dance or maybe take a nap. By remembering the Love of God, judgment subsides. (It isn't fun, anyway.) We don't want to block the love anymore. Judgment is a defense against love. I don't want to defend against God anymore. Do you? I don't want to block the experience of God's Love and Joy. When we let go of judging the circumstances of our lives, we learn that every situation arises to teach us we are All Innocent. Will we defend against the world we see, or ask love to interpret for us? By letting go of the meaning we have given to the situations in our lives we can receive the gifts they bestow upon us. By letting go of the "good-bad" perspective and staying willing to learn from Divine Love we have set the goal of love. We aren't limiting our learning to outcomes based on our past choices.

When I was eighteen and leaving home for college, I thought I was losing something. Instead of being happy about moving forward to the next life chapter and receiving a college education, I had a drama about leaving behind my high school boyfriend. Letting go of my high school boyfriend was the only thing I could see. My self-concept was associated with the high school romance. My departure for college felt like separation from my identity. Change seemed terrifying. I was crying and carrying on in the family's driveway. Chris, my nine-year-old brother said, "We all have to grow up sometime." That put an immediate end to my tantrum. If my parents had said the same thing, it would have meant nothing to me at the time. But for my little brother to say it, snapped me into reality. *We all have to grow up sometime.* A short time later, I broke up with the high school boyfriend. Life moves forward. I often forget what caused my big upsets. But I remember what healed them. The Truth heals every upset.

"Truth will correct all errors in my mind."
ACIM Workbook Lesson 107

We can't see the future. It probably won't be exactly what we imagine it will be. Chris is not a cop, and he is not an alligator. I never fulfilled my second grade aspiration of becoming a go-go dancer. (I'm not sure whether my parents were relieved when I announced in sixth grade that I would be a musician!) When we give our faith to God, we are giving our faith to that which knows more than we do at this time.

God sees the *Real* You!

It's relaxing to place our faith in the Love of God. We aren't putting off joy until an imagined future. Our plans might change anyway. We free ourselves from pretending. It isn't fun to think we know everything. We were wrong anyway! When we *really* decide to grow up, we let go of believing the outside world is the source of our joy. The choice for the Love of God means we are letting go of insisting on another source.

Are you willing to experience your True Self? God created Us Innocent and Good. We can hold on to meaningless concepts about the self to delay our awakening, but awakening to our True Self is inevitable. As we let go of our little images of the self, we are letting go of nothing in order to welcome Our True Selves. If we look at a photograph of ourselves, we are aware the photograph is not really us. The photograph is a likeness. Our personalities are also symbols of us. Our thoughts about our separate selves are images we made—just like photographs. When we judge someone, we are not seeing the Truth about them, we are seeing a symbol we made of them. God did not make the unloving thoughts we are thinking. God does not judge.

One day I picked up a newspaper and started reading an editorial. The editorial pointed out badness—badness in the world and goodness. It was written from a perception of moral goodness at the expense of another's badness. Separation leapt out of the words. As I read the editorial, I noticed that my awareness began to shift. My mind was being altered for me. The Pamela person wasn't doing anything other than reading a newspaper.

"Now you need but to remember you need do NOTHING. It would be far more profitable now merely to concentrate on this than to consider what you SHOULD do."
ACIM 18.VIII.67

My eyes were open. I was not even meditating. Pamela the body, the personality, was not altering my mind. By doing *A Course in Miracles* with great willingness, I had given permission for my mind, my perceptions, to be altered, to be healed. The Spirit of Love to which I give great willingness was altering my perception. The Spirit of Love is in everything. I sat down and shut my eyes, allowing the healing of my perceptions to continue. I became aware the opinions in the editorial were judgments. They were MY judgments projected out into the world and into a newspaper editorial. My hidden unloving thoughts were being mirrored back to me. Next, I became aware that they were my judgments about ME.

Ruh-Roh!

I sat there and did not interfere. From deep within my Mind, I heard Spirit say, "Those aren't *My* Thoughts." *A Course in Miracles* trains our mind to give up judgment. We can't really judge; even our ability to judge is an illusion. We don't recognize what anything is for because we do not see the Universal Plan. Our natural ability to see the Whole Plan is blocked from our awareness by the illusion of separate interests.

The *Course* doesn't take away our views and leave us with nothing. The *ego beliefs* are nothing. As we let them go, our mind is liberated. We are free to experience love in everything, everywhere, all the time. By giving our trust to the Loving Mind, we discover that our judgments are just a bunch of nonsense. God loves us. God loves everyone. The *Course* gives us specific guidance for practice. We learn to recognize the Truth. The *Course* gives us lessons in natural vision.

> *"Real vision is not only unlimited by space and distance,*
> *but it does not depend on the body's eyes at all."*
>
> *ACIM Workbook Lesson 30*

We learn how to see God in everything because we allow the self-imposed obstacles to be undone. Love is already here. Peace is already here. Joy is already here. God hasn't gone away. We are learning to let go of the self-imposed blocks to love, peace and joy. We are relinquishing our defenses against God. (Hint: *this is a major point!*) A *Course in Miracles* teaches us to question what we see with our eyes; question what we believe. The Text tells us, *"Questioning illusions is the first step in undoing them. The miracle, or the 'right answer,' corrects them"* (ACIM 3.V.32). As we question our unloving thoughts, we are withdrawing our faith in them.

In the situation in which I was reading the newspaper and noticed judgment, my healing did not stop with noticing the other person's judgment. I was not "innocent" because of the other person's judgment. That would have been the false innocence that the ego takes from believing it can get "goodness" or "being all right" at the expense of another being "wrong." That is not healing; it's the ego's short term investment in winning. FALSE innocence is the "look how holy I am" belief in separation. When the ego "wins" control of our minds, we are in hell; we lose the experience of Heaven.

The Universal Happiness Plan is also a Process. We have some illusions in our perfectly created minds blocking the experience of love, joy, peace and innocence. What comes into our lives comes because we have called. We call for love to heal our minds of the blocks. Our deepest will is joy.

What isn't real has come to heal.

Our judgments, our unloving thoughts, are the concepts we make up about the perfect, united, Loving Self. We all make the same mistake (believe in separation). All dark spots of (seeming) separation transform in the same way (forgiveness). When we are willing to see the Truth, the Wholeness Truth and nothing but the Truth, we give our illusions to the Light. Willingness directs our mind to shift from trusting our illusions to trusting the love within. Shifts are miracles. We are learning to trust our Holy Loving Self.

PRACTICE:

I call to mind someone with whom I share a negative bond.

(Yes them.)

In this moment, I let go of the story.

Surrender does not mean loss.

I am ready to drop my resistance to the Love and Light of God.

I am willing to stop using this person as a human shield against the experience of God's Presence.

Now, I enter deeper into the light of truth.

I accept the holy light of truth and allow it to shine into my awareness.

There is nothing I have to do but offer my willingness.

This light is blessing me.

Now I extend the light to the person I called into this practice.

I bless them with the holy light of truth.

The light is transforming our bond and blessing us both.

I tell them, "The light has come."

They are now telling me, "The light has come."

We are joined with and by eternal love.

God created us as One.

It is with gratitude and humility that I remember this now.

Innocence is natural because I am still as God created me.

This reminds me of the eternal innocence of my brother/
sister.

Our innocence is shared.

We sit in this light for as long as feels natural.

Amen.

Notice Your Defenses:

The "S!@#$%&=!" Word*

The Holy Spirit does not force the truth on us. But eventually, something happens at the level of form to increase our willingness to wake up. The Holy Spirit is the Spiritual Teacher given to us by God. Our Spiritual Teacher motivates us using the highly individualized curriculums of our lives. On a sunny afternoon in Florida, I was enjoying a smoothie with a friend. We were relaxed and happy. With no warning, she mentioned our impending birthdays. Until that moment, it had not occurred to me I would turn fifty that year. I stopped mid-slurp. Instantly, I consoled myself with ancient Mayan prophesies. The world would end in 2012.

Problem solved.
But not really.

I did some serious soul searching. Why was I so concerned? Was it about my body? I *knew* what was sounding the alarm. When we look within, we are *all* familiar with our blocks already. They aren't new. We put them there ourselves. We make them up and scare ourselves. Then we *keep* our scary, made-up thoughts by hiding them. But they don't stay hidden. The not-so-smoothie incident was well after becoming an ardent student of *A Course in Miracles*. I was already a devoted student of the *Course* by my thirtieth birthday when Marianne Williamson appeared on the Oprah Winfrey show. But the impending world-ending birthday sang a shocking wake-up song into my heart. *No more delay!* After decades of studying and *(I thought)* even applying the *Course*, nasty life issues still clung to me like deer ticks.

S!@#$%&=!*
My motivation was seriously increased.

"Increasing motivation for change in the learner is all that a teacher need do to guarantee change. This is because a change in motivation is a change of mind, and this will inevitably produce fundamental change because the mind is fundamental."

ACIM 6.b.72

I would keep no fear thought unhealed! Time had ended for my resistance. Now I would look at the parts of my mind that I had hidden. I would even ponder my most dreaded word in *A Course in Miracles*:

Salvation.
(Cue scary organ music!)

I always experienced such a charge around the "*S!@#$%*&=!* word" that I had skipped those parts of the book. That word always seemed so Christian-y; so church-y; so *being-forced-to-go-to-the-Methodist-church-against-my-will-when-I-was-growing-up-y*. I was *doing just fine* studying *A Course in Miracles* for over two decades without paying attention to the salvation parts! Thank you very much! Nobody could make me read anything or do anything against my will now! (And I won't eat lima beans either.)

They were wrong, and I was right...
...except that I still perceived life issues as sucking away at my happiness.

Okay, what if I *peeked* at the *Course* teachings about salvation? I could read the salvation parts without going to any church or eating any beans.

After all, the world might be ending.
I definitely was turning fifty.

So, I vowed to go all the way (minus beans and church). When I opened my mind to the word, one of my friends piped in, "Oh, to me, 'Salvation' means my good." Suddenly, I relaxed. When I open my mind, peace is there. My big defense story over a word meant nothing. The "salvation" word was only ink on paper. The ink sat there, minding its own business. *I* was the one getting all preachy and judgmental.

Ink can't hurt me.

If a word (or situation) holds a charge for us, we are defending. We are defending against Truth. We are loved and safe already. When we are defending, we are trying to keep ourselves safe by inappropriate means. We are guarding our hearts *against* love, against peace. The emotional charge attacks our awareness of peace. As we put our dukes down, love comes in and gently corrects our perceptions. We learn that love is here by relaxing when we feel the charge. We cultivate a long-term relationship with love by trusting on purpose. *Remember:* our fear-based emotions are not healed by pushing them down, but by relaxing in their presence. It is not necessary to know what will happen next in the world of form. (We don't have a clue. Just ask the Mayans.) Moment by moment, we trust peace Itself.

God = Love = Peace

I started noticing my defenses. When I was prompted do something and my reaction was *"NOT that!"* I stopped and observed. I saw the reacting "I" was the ego trying to save *itself.* The ego wanted to save itself from love.

Gasp!

The ego has a plan for salvation. So does God. Guess what—they are the opposite.

So ... wait a minute.

My *good,* my *safety,* my actual *life* does not depend on NOT EATING LIMA BEANS? This is just a meaningless rule I had invented as a child? Where were my other rules? I started looking at my made-up, meaningless, old rules and their outcomes. By observing my defenses, I noticed *what* was defending. The defensive little ego is insecure because it isn't a fully developed thought system. It is only an impermanent belief, an image of a self. The ego is a bunch of nonsense. God didn't create it.

PRACTICE:

Where are your old rules?

Where is there an emotional charge?

What beliefs are you defending?

What conditions have you made for your happiness?

As I pondered my list of old rules, I noticed my church = guilt story. THEY (my thoughts about my childhood church) called me a guilty sinner. I told myself I could save myself from this guilt by *judging back* and never returning! *So there! Hi-yah!!* But that old strategy did not put me into contact with a current *experience* of innocence. Whenever I thought about church, the *emotional energy* I experienced was guilt. Was a now retired (or dead) minister guilty? Had God created a bad little Pamela? No. *My* decision to *keep* "church = guilt" thoughts made me *feel* guilty.

> *"You may not realize that the ego has set up a plan for salvation in opposition to God's. It is this plan in which you believe."*
>
> ACIM Workbook Lesson 71

"Church = guilt" was a made-up old rule.
The ego made it up.

It did not matter whether anyone in the past (including me) condemned me. The present perception of guilt attacks the mind that holds it. By defending my "little self" in my mind, I was attacking my own peace of mind by attacking the awareness of *eternal* safety and innocence.

"If you did not feel guilty, you could not attack, for condemnation is the root of attack. It is the judgment of one mind by another as unworthy of love and deserving of punishment."

ACIM 11.X.85

When we defend, we are reinforcing the belief that we are vulnerable. By choosing the ego's plan, we uphold our belief in the made-up, frail self. Guilt, attack and faith-in-weakness travel together, weaving the tapestry of the ego identity. The ego's interpretation of my childhood experience at church was just that—a child's interpretation. I might be wrong. (!!!) *(The ego hates when you admit the possibility of wrongness.)* Perhaps nobody called me a guilty sinner. From where I sit today, I cannot be sure. I can tell you—we are never angry at a fact. Anger arises from allowing the ego to interpret for us. The Holy Spirit will interpret every situation for us with our permission. Today, I allow my emotions without placing my faith in the storyline. I give my trust to the Holy Spirit. The Holy Spirit knows the difference between fact (love) and fiction (illusion). I have shared this example from my life, but the lesson is universally applicable. It applies to church as much as it applies to lima beans.

During the purification process, we look at our thoughts with the Holy Spirit. Our Right Mind (Holy Spirit) separates the loving thoughts from the illusions. The Holy Spirit is the "wisdom to know the difference." When we *justify* our unloving thoughts, the ego is in story-telling mode. The false self is declaring its interpretations as "right" and a person or circumstance as "wrong." Guilt stories are the central theme of the ego's plan for salvation. The ego tells us that if someone or something outside us would just *change already*, or *not change*, we would be happy and filled with peace. *They* are keeping it from us. (Oh, poor us, and mean, powerful them.) If God's Plan for Salvation is the *opposite* of guilt, this could only mean one thing:

Our Grievances Don't Amount to a Hill of Beans.

Grievances are nothing but our own fearful interpretations designed to keep us from *experiencing* our good. We made them up ourselves. God's Plan for Salvation is all about forgiving and being happy, loving and free. If you are ever doing a crossword puzzle and you are looking for a five-letter word for God's Plan for Salvation, try this: relax. Don't you feel better already? If you are looking for a seven-letter word, try this one: forgive. (I started with relax because the ego defends against forgiveness.)

By deciding to relax and follow God's Plan for Salvation, I found a much easier path. I was choosing the Sane Master. Moment by moment, I can choose love as my Guide. Following *this* Guide, I discovered startling information about my Self. It turns out those external things I believed so fiercely that I needed to be safe, to be okay, to be loved, were not the Real Source of my safety, my acceptability or my love. By following God's Plan, I freed the world from *my* plans. By accepting God's Will as the Source of my happiness, I could extend the happiness that already dwells within.

The even bigger surprise was that I didn't need to *do* anything, *have* anything or *be approved by* anyone. These made-up safety rules were meaningless. God does not make conditions for Loving. The ego does. The ego's list is end-less. My ego had invented a list of conditions under which I would allow myself to feel loved, safe and acceptable. I could win international awards, be a good-good girl, pro-mote world peace, and work long hours for free. Still, the ego would declare me *not good enough.* The ego is incapable of love. The ego's rule is:

MORE.

See that little spot over there? THERE was the proof of my guilt. That's what the ego is always looking for—evi-dence of guilt. I attempted to outrun my self-judgment by trying with all of my little might. But my little self could never do enough. I studied *A Course in Miracles* for hours every day. My brain quoted sections on cue. Surely God (I mean people, I mean God) would love me then. Surely other people loving me enough would mean I was lovable enough.

Then a beautiful thing happened. By giving my willing-ness to let go of the ego's plan for salvation and accept God's Plan instead, I started seeing things differently. I started rec-ognizing what I was doing. I saw that *I was doing this to myself.* People (God seriously bless them) started showing me the absolute futility of the ego's plan. I saw that the ego's evi-dence was false—false evidence.

While minding my own business, living my life, I attracted people who lost their minds on me. They would freak out, telling me of my guilt. The lesson was perfectly constructed so I could allow my perception to shift. I recog-nized that *even in the material form of the storyline,* I was inno-cent. While people projected their guilt stories onto me,

I had no reaction. There was no stuffing of emotion. My mind shifted from victim to Vulcan. *Guilt is highly illogical.* I saw the other people's innocence too.

Bam!
I had chosen God's Plan for Salvation—The Universal Happiness Plan.

The people were telling me (yelling to me) *my* subconscious belief in guilt and... (drum roll please) the belief no longer held any power over me. I no longer had any faith in it. Guilt is an idea, *not* a fact. As long as guilt held a charge for me, anyone who came along and projected their subconscious belief in guilt onto me was also projecting *my* subconscious belief in guilt.

There is no separation.

"When I am healed, I am not healed alone."
ACIM Workbook Lesson 137

In a moment of insanity, one person remaining awake and remembering the truth is enough. Love transforms the ego's pain and guilt plan into God's Universal Happiness Plan. The mind is saved from the belief in guilt and returned to the unconditional Love of God.

Only the love is real.

God is unconditional love.

Love that is *conditional* is not real.

It's a defense against God.

The outside world shows up as we ask on the *inside*. Situations prove to us what we believe. The physical world is *"the witness to your state of mind, the outside picture of an inward condition"* (ACIM 21.1.1). Every person or circumstance comes into our life to bring our thoughts into conscious awareness. In plain sight, we can see the thoughts we have been empowering. Do we want to keep them? Maybe a thought is true, maybe not. *(Hint: ego thoughts are not true and make us unhappy.)* If we knew the difference between fact and fiction, we would be consistently happy.

When we are willing to question our beliefs, we ask the Holy Spirit if they are true. Seeing our hidden thoughts by the light of the Holy Spirit is enlightening. The thoughts are no longer hiding in the dark. In any moment, we can let our meaningless thoughts be lifted. Any person or situation on our *S!@#* (BLEEP) list is really on our *S!@#$%*&=!* (SALVATION) list. God's Salvation Plan is well structured and carefully planned for the happiness of everyone.

The ego's plan is undone by our willingness to put all guilt and misery into the Hands of Love. This is also called the Atonement. *A Course in Miracles* says accepting the Atonement for ourselves is our *sole function*. I read that for years. It seemed important, but I didn't understand what it meant. When I opened my mind to salvation, I started to notice "Atonement" sounded just like "Salvation." I asked another one of my friends about it. She looked up "Atonement" in the Robert Perry *Glossary of Terms* and said, "It says, *'See Salvation!'*" Next, I realized the *Course* says Atonement and Healing are not related, *they are identical.* So Salvation, Atonement and Healing are all the same thing.

What a relief!

I didn't need to do anything religious or fancy or complicated. My sole function—your sole function—is to *accept* healing. Our part is tiny. The love is here right now. We do nothing in this Plan; we *stop* doing. Our job is to stop defending and *accept* the love that never left.

(Thank You, Jesus.)

The belief in guilt is being undone in our precious Mind. We are letting go of the plan for separation and attack and joining the Spirit of Joy that loves us unconditionally. By surrendering our Minds to Love, we are joining the Plan that works. We are allowing our own healing. God's Plan will work; ours won't. Once we stop defending our unworkable beliefs, The Plan is fun. (Pinky swear.) Guilt will not save you. What...you're insulted now? You *aren't* attracted to guilt? OK. So what is your problem, your issue? How does it make your feel? (ANOTHER HINT: the *issue* isn't causing the emotion. The problem is an effect. You have faith in the problem because you identified with guilt first. The ego plays the opposite game. It's so immature.)

EXAMPLE: do you feel guilty because you can't pay your bills? Your ego mind's belief in guilt has attracted the situation called "can't pay them." Now the ego is having a field day. Woo-hoo! Look at the guilty "me" who can't pay the bills. Did God create this? What "makes" you feel guilty? What if you were willing to let the Holy Spirit heal you of the belief in guilt? WARNING: this involves letting go of the belief in guilt everywhere, throughout space and time. (Yes, I am referring to the seven-letter word—forgive.) Don't worry. The Holy Spirit is good at this. The Holy Spirit knows that guilt is not real. You can just sit there and be willing. You don't even have to do push-ups or crunches. If you don't like lima beans, you don't have to eat them. (If you are willing to see them as innocent, The Holy Spirit will take it from there.)

The Universal Happiness Plan features letting go of our meaningless *(totally made up by the ego and not true; nothing)* subconscious belief we are guilty. If we knew how unconditionally lovable we already are, we wouldn't invent a list of conditions. We would not place a list of demands. "I demand the *world* prove to me I am lovable, safe and acceptable because I do not feel that way inside. Here is my list of outer conditions for security." We make up this list (also called the ego's plan) and give it meaning. It is our mental list of "need to have or can't have" in order to be happy, safe and lovable list. It actually means nothing because it is NOT part of God's Universal Plan.

Once we relax into our unconditional lovability, we recognize our natural safety. We are identifying with the Eternal Truth. We only defend when we sense danger. The mental weapons we invent to keep us "safe" are double-edged swords. Our ego minds use them against ourselves. They attract evidence to support our false belief that we need them. (We don't.)

What scares you?

Why do you perceive you are in danger?

Stop right now and be honest with yourself.

I'll wait.

What if there is nothing to fear?

What if you stopped wanting your fear thoughts?

What if you wanted God instead?

"Blessed are those who have not seen and yet have believed."
(John 20:29)

For a long time, my hairstyle was short except for one long "tail" in the back. One day, I decided to update my hairstyle. The hairdresser told me the first step was to cut off the ponytail. Even though I knew he was speaking the truth, a small tear ran down my cheek when he picked up the scissors. I had a thought in my head about the hair on my head. (It only hurt for a minute.) Even when we recognize our illusions to be fear thoughts, we still might encounter fear of healing. Why? We are in transition. We are awakening from our old thought system. The truth is not yet visible. We are learning to trust the process.

I used to reach the part in the purification process where I could see the issue, but feared letting go. Eventually, I became willing to ask my Holy Self *why* I was afraid of healing. Who would I be without the pain? Life had been chugging along with the issue. I was in a long-term relationship with the problem. We had a history. I knew what to expect. What if the misery *dis*-appeared and there was nothing underneath but a big hole? I might disappear!

I who?

Whose plan was this? Who identifies with the problems? (ANSWER: ego.) The Holy Spirit is the bridge that leads our awareness back to love. As I take my faith away from fear and place my faith in the Spirit of Love, I gain confidence. Each step in my journey confirms this confidence. There are no holes in the bridge to God. Step by step I acknowledge the holiness in those around me, beyond every material circumstance. Wholeness returns to my awareness. The journey is a voyage of recognition. We are safe in God already.

PRACTICE:

Imagine how it would feel to go about the rest of your day knowing you are unconditionally loved and safe. Visualize your day being perfectly planned for you by the universal love that is your happiness. Don't imagine details of this day (yet). Just allow the sensation of the happiest, safest, most peaceful day you have ever lived. You are not in charge of the decisions for this day. They are being made by the Source of Happiness Itself. Relax into this sensation for a few moments. Remember that you are loved. Open your mind and receive inspiration from the Source of Love.

Notice what thoughts come up for you now.

REMEMBER TO LAUGH

GOD BELIEVES IN BILL MAHER

Bill Maher does not believe in God. He says so all the time. He even made a whole movie about it. But God *does* believe in Bill Maher. We believe in what we create. That's how creation works. We have thoughts, trust them, create with them. I just imagined that sentence and typed it.

Voilà!
Bill Maher sure thinks about God a lot.

Even though Bill Maher thinks about God a lot, he did not create God. God created Bill Maher. God created Bill Maher even though Bill Maher doesn't believe in God. Technically, God *knows* Bill Maher. We don't all believe the same thing. Have you noticed? We all have our own convictions. In our fragmented state, we invent different stuff and trust what we made up, even if nobody else does. Our inventions seem true to us. (It even seems true that we are fragmented.) We think thoughts without God and then trust them. We make up weird stuff and convince ourselves it's true. *A Course in Miracles* calls this "hallucinating" or "having an illusion."

When we take our illusions seriously, we scare ourselves. We imagine that we have really done something deserving punishment. Once we realize that it's a hallucination, we stop scaring ourselves and think something else. When we are Thinking with God, it might appear that we are believing different things, but we really aren't. When we are Thinking with God, we are all Thinking the same thing because we are loving, no matter what it looks like on the outside. Love is the Truth.

WorldColor was an artistic affirmation of Native American prophecies. According to the prophecies, when the four races of people (black, red, yellow and white) come together, there will be a great society and peace on earth. The people in the rock band represented the four races of humankind. (These races look different on the outside. The musicians just wanted to play music because it was how we expressed our joy.)

I traveled around to various Indian reservations in search of the tribal origins of the prophecies. The Hopi elder said, "This is our prophecy. Take it around the world with your music." The Lakota elder said, "This is our prophecy. Take it around the world with your music." That kept happening. I was glad the elders liked the music. But I kept getting the same response. Then I met an Algonquin woman named Bluebird Woman who had the same vision. So I came out and asked, "Bluebird Woman, why do these tribes all have the same vision?" She said, "Because it's the truth."

Whether the truth is coming from different tribes, different editions of A Course in Miracles or different theologies, races or faces, the truth is still true. The truth is unalterable. Joni Mitchell said, "Love has many faces." It's still Love. We are still Love because we are still as God created us. (God Loves Joni Mitchell. I do not know whether Bill Maher believes in Joni Mitchell, knows her or appears to like her.)

Love is the One Truth that Created and knows us, no matter what we believe. And we can imagine some strange stuff! No matter what illusions we have, we are still Thoughts of God, Loved in the Mind of our One Creator. At any moment in which we are forgetting the truth, the truth is not forgetting us. No matter how much we are hallucinating, we are still in the Mind of God.

> "The physical world exists only because man can use it to correct his unbelief, which placed him in it originally."
> ACIM 1.1 Miracle Principle 51

Sometimes people read *A Course in Miracles* and get upset because the *Course* says that God doesn't know we are here in the world. It offends them. They assume the *Course* is telling them that God doesn't know where they are. We are the ones who don't remember where *we* are. Everyone is in God's Mind all the time. God has never lost track of us. God loves Bill Maher even though Bill Maher does not believe in God. God does not even have any of our "not God" thoughts because those "not God" thoughts aren't even real. Thank God, that God can't hallucinate. This comforts me. I am happy God can't hallucinate. I am happy that no matter how many weird thoughts I dream up, God loves me and God loves Bill Maher (and Joni Mitchell). This helps me because I like to laugh at the thoughts that aren't real.

Here in what appears to be time, I can use my experiences to recognize how hilarious my "not God" thoughts have been. When I am not joyful, I can remember that I am hallucinating and surrender my unloving ("not God") thoughts for correction. Any space-time experience can teach me if I am willing to let my "not God" thoughts be transformed. Sometimes people see paradoxes in the *Course* and then they either get angry at the book or they fight with each other. This is so funny. It is even funnier than Bill Maher. *A Course in Miracles* is a course in mind training. Mind training is built right into the book. Every time I appear to see a paradox, I can choose.

When I let go of ink and paper and shift to the peace inside my Self, the mind training is moving forward. (Choo! Choo!) But if I use the ink and paper as an excuse to view someone as wrong and me as right, I am stalling out on the tracks. I am looking at the form and making it more important than the message (content). The *Course* gives the message over and over again. (Choose! Choose! Choose!) We keep being told that we are all innocent and to value only love. The Universal Experience is an adventure in unlearning the value that we have placed on everything other than love, peace and joy. We unlearn our false values by looking at them and remembering what a joke they are. We look at them and recognize they are valueless. *A Course in Miracles* is brilliant and hilarious.

The Holy Spirit understands that we trust our "not God" thoughts because we made them up. The Holy Spirit isn't fooled by our unloving thoughts and does not mind taking this stuff off our hands. The Holy Spirit is in charge of ridding our minds of these "not God" thoughts (with our permission). God does not even believe in the stuff at all. God is like a reverse atheist. God loves Bill Maher, but God does not even know that Bill Maher does not believe in God. The Holy Spirit can see our "not God," unloving thoughts and waits for us to be done with them. It's the Holy Spirit's job to purify our minds, and that's why there is no order of difficulty in miracles. The Holy Spirit has complete faith in *us* and no faith in our fear. The Holy Spirit knows our "not God" thoughts are not real.

The Holy Spirit doesn't take away our loveless beliefs and leave us sitting there with nothing. Love reveals to us that our opinions meant nothing. Miracles liberate our minds so we can experience the love that already is everything, everywhere, all the time, beyond time and space. As we forgive, our ego thought system is undone. Eternal Love rises into awareness. By looking within, we are joining our minds with God and with everyone. There is One Truth in every mind because Love is Truth. We are letting go of the "not God" belief that there are separate Truths. Love, happiness and peace are making a comeback in our consciousness. Reggae musicians have been singing this message for a long time. People all over the world love reggae.

Bill Maher probably likes reggae too.
Amen.

OPEN YOUR HEART

CATS, CLOWNS AND CRICKETS

I used to be afraid of clowns. Am I the only one? A scary clown lived in the closet when I was a child. But Divine, Eternal Love is in my mind. There is a perfect Plan for me to remember that I Am that love. There is a Plan for me to remember the Divine Love in everyone and everything. So I grew up and Divine Love sent a friendly clown into my life to heal the fear.

My clown friend and I met years ago at an arts conference where we were promoting our shows. This good-natured clown performs children's shows with his wife, who has also become my lifelong friend. My clown friend's wife designs costumes and dresses up in them. She is also a dancer. She dances around in lifelike costumes. Her costumes are larger-than-life replicas of…

bugs.

God sent a clown and a bug dancer to teach me I can love bugs and I can love clowns. Now I even have a picture of a clown on my refrigerator and a picture of a bug. God is in everything. It is our purpose to remember that. One year on April 1, my clown friend came to town and wanted to get together for dinner. I thought, "This must be a trick. I am going out to dinner with my clown friend on April Fool's Day." But he was perfectly well-behaved. Clowns aren't scary and neither are bugs. They're fun. I know that now. I am so grateful that I am not using clowns and bugs to block happiness from my God-created mind anymore. God has always been in my Mind. God has always been in clowns and God has always been in bugs. God is Love without an opposite. Clowns and bugs have always been fun.

Just ask my cat.

My cat really enjoys playing with bugs. Usually, I can't even detect the bug with my physical eyes. My cat has the vision to see the bug. He can entertain himself and have lots of fun with a bug that is invisible to me. The fun is easy to see. In the past, I didn't like cats. I identified myself as a "dog person" and didn't realize you could love both dogs and cats. My intellect would agree with you that God is in everything. But part of me thought you had to pick a side.

I thought there were "dog people" and "cat people." The belief in a "good side" and a "bad side" was a projected untrue thought about myself. I had not yet gone deep enough. The Whole Love of God is in me. I'm in It and so is everything and everyone. God was still in me when I "was only a dog person." I just didn't know it yet. Even when we can't perceive the Whole Love, God can see it. The love is still there.

When part of our mind is opposing the truth of our wholeness, we project the resistance to love and pick sides. We tell ourselves that God wants our team to win, not *their* team. We even pray for our team to win and don't even get our own joke. But the God Mind inside knows the Truth.

When I believed that only dogs could be lovable, I was believing something that was not true. My heart had not yet opened to cats. God was already in cats, but I didn't know it yet. I had not yet gone deep enough into my belief that God is Love without an opposite. I had not yet healed my resistance to love.

Love wanted me to experience Itself in cats so It started sending a series of dreams. Sometimes Divine Self does that. We can hear from Divine Self in our night dreams. Divine Love communicates with us in lots of ways. One way is in our dreams. In the dreams, a cat was coming to live with me. The dreams kept coming. Divine Love is a great communicator and really wanted me to get the message. Divine Love already knows that It's in everything, including us. Love wants us to recognize Our Self. So Divine Love is persistent.

My dog at the time had a lifelong ambition to get up close and personal with a cat. Cats never seemed to take it the right way. They would always run away. Around this time, it was getting near the end of my dog's earthly incarnation. One day, my dog and I were taking a slow walk around the block. A cat walked right up to my dog and sniffed her right where animals sniff each other! My dog turned around, and they were nose-to-nose. My dog finally made friends with a cat! If she could do it, so could I. The cat gave my dog happiness in that moment. My opinion about cats changed.

When my dog passed away, I did not run right out and adopt another dog. I waited. One day I went to the beach, and a text came to my phone. The text was a photo of a little orange kitten with a message saying the kitten needed a home. I was sitting with a friend but mentioned nothing to her. She started talking about winning a sand sculpture contest. She said the sand sculpture she built was a cat on a phone! Divine Love sends us messages in lots of ways. Sometimes Divine Love sends text messages through one friend and then talks through the mouth of another friend. It sends dreams. (Sometimes it sniffs a butt.) Divine Love is always communicating with us. We can receive the messages if we are willing. It's up to us to follow the instructions.

This self-proclaimed "dog person" adopted the kitten and fell in Love. Divine Love sent a kitten to open my heart to what was already true. God is in cats and God is in dogs. God is in clowns and bugs. We are all on the same team because the Love of God is shared. If I withhold Love anywhere, then I forget that I am Love without an opposite. I told my cat, "I love you. You made me a cat lover." The God in my mind had been a cat lover all along. My cat helped me to remember the Divine Love already within. I didn't know a cat would help me remember the God in me. My willingness to listen to the messages and follow the instructions opened me to Love. Only our willingness is necessary because love without an opposite is already in our minds. Next, I helped my cat realize he is a dog lover. And then my cat helped two dogs become cat lovers. Love abounds! Boundless love was already in our minds, but The Universal Happiness Plan sent us to each other to remember together.

Who has The Plan sent to you?

Divine Love has a perfect Plan for all of us to recognize the Love of God in everyone and everything. When we shut our hearts, The Plan will send us a cat, a clown, or something else to bug us until we decide we want to remember and love. We can open our hearts because God *is* in us ... We have unlimited help because we have the power of

God willing us to remember. Love is our Superpower. When we feel the ache of our own closed heart, the pain is not coming from outside. We like to pretend it's coming from the world. But is isn't. The pain is never coming from a cat or a clown or a bug. Some beings find bugs tasty and fun. The pain is never coming from ... the pain is not coming from ... the pain is not coming from ... (Take a breath.)

Did a person or a situation just come to mind?

The pain comes from closing our hearts. When we close our hearts, the Love of God can't flow through. God is still in our mind, but we are the ones stepping on the hose, blocking the flow. Are we willing to trust God more than what our physical eyes are showing us? Are we willing to deepen our faith? This does not mean we believe we will get our way at the level of form, but that we trust God's Way. Our faith is deeper than our storyline. We admit we don't know everything. We are not in charge of the Divine Plan but are fully blessed by it. We open to receive the grace available in the present. The Love of God is available no matter what our conditions look like. Sometimes I have to go really deep. I have to remind myself that getting angry will not protect me. Pushing anger down won't either. Our True Protection is One Who knows there is nothing to fear. Fear is a call to turn the mind back to Love.

PRAYER:

Spirit of Love,

I will not protect myself here. Hold my hand. I am willing. I will not defend myself. I'm not handling this. If you want me to do something or say something, I will do or say exactly what you tell me to do or say. You are in charge. Walk me through this. Cast out the illusion of fear from my heart. I only want You—Your Love—the Truth. I want Your Will.

I let go of my ideas of what it looks like. I want to experience Your Love above all else. I will go as deep as necessary. Here is my faith. I am willing to see whatever you show me.

I Trust You.

Amen.

Fear doesn't come from God. When there's fear, it's only because I have resisted God. I have judged something inaccurately. The only correct judgment is innocence. By welcoming God back into my awareness, I am admitting I was wrong in my perception of something. Now, I would rather have the love in my mind. Peace returns. When we want to hear from the God Mind we can because it's God's Will. By aligning our will with God's Will, we can accept the help that's available for us. As we practice listening to God's Voice and following God's Voice, our trust strengthens. We are practicing and we have the strength of unlimited Holiness supporting every step.

Sometimes our God Mind will tell us "no." It will never tell us "no" means guilt. Sometimes "no" is the most loving answer. Our God Mind is teaching us that love is in everyone and everything, so the message is always innocence. Sometimes the answer is, "No to that action or form." Other times the message is, "Not yet; by the way, I love you." Our God Mind will teach us how to communicate lovingly with each other too. We learn that approval isn't love because approval has an opposite and can change back and forth between approval and disapproval. Our God Mind is inside us and never stops loving us. Once we recognize that approval isn't love, it becomes easier to communicate "no" respectfully when "no" is the loving answer. We learn how to communicate fearlessly by deepening our communion with the Voice of God. The Voice of God is our Teacher.

Once, the Teacher guided me to say "no" to a particular form in a relationship. The person was mad at me. They disapproved of the answer "no" and wanted me to say, "Yes." I kept praying about it, but the answer was still "no," so I asked for emotional help with the situation. The next day, I was about to take a nap and went to set a radio alarm clock. I usually set the radio alarm clock on a music station. While I was trying to change the time on the alarm, the radio dial turned to a Christian station and would not turn off. Short of unplugging the radio, the only thing I could do was listen to the message.

Here is what the man on the radio said: *"Ask for what to do and follow through. Do you have faith that Christ loves you? How does this apply in your life right now? Forgive someone who is not forgiving you. Love someone who is not forgiving you."* That was the emotional help I needed. It worked. It put my heart back in contact with what was not visible to my earthly eyes. I remembered the unlimited Love of God we all share. I felt it. Eventually, the other person felt it too.

When we open our heart-minds, we can recognize the Shared Love of God shining all around us. We are given the ears to hear and the eyes to see. The God Mind wants us to recognize our Innocent Self in everything. We have to look beyond the surface. We have the x-ray vision of love because love is our True Self. It's safe to accept the love that's here right now. So if The Universal Happiness Plan has sent a clown into your life and it's bugging you, it's not a catastrophe...

(I couldn't help it; my clown friend made me do it.)

It's not a catastrophe. It's Unlimited Love giving you the grace, the opportunity to go deeper and recognize Your Divine Self. Don't you want that? I do. We all deserve to experience the Love in everything. Only our willingness is necessary.

SHIFT TO NEUTRAL

DO ASK. DON'T TELL.

We have all heard, "Ask and you shall receive." Do we ask or do we tell? When we're telling God what we want, giving our list of what we think we need to be happy, we aren't asking. We're telling God our *honey-do* list. Do this. Do that, and I will be happy. Sometimes we add creative visualization. We see ourselves as already having what we imagine we need in order to be happy. *We will use the Power of Attraction!*

Next, we complain:

"God didn't do what I told Him to do. God is not co-operating with my plan. Why, oh why hasn't my prayer been answered? I've asked, visualized, affirmed in the present tense. Why am I still so tense?!" We assume we haven't received.

Have we asked or have we told?

While telling God our plans, we placed limits on receiving. (Oops!) Our minds were closed against hearing. We wanted our little, tiny separate will to be done. We imagined that our will *could* be separate from God's Will (and *better*). When we told our Creator what He should do for us to make us happy, we were placing demands. "Make me happy God!" (with something outside). By doing this, we imagine *ourselves* outside God.

Perhaps we don't *appear* to pray that way (anymore). Our powerful minds *are* always attracting. Pretty, creative visualizations of what we assume will make us happy attract form. *Stuffed fear attracts too.* We are *always* making images of our thoughts. When we decide we want something in the world to make us happy, we are forgetting that what we *really* want is happiness. God is Happiness and we are One with God. Any time we look to the world for our happiness and peace, we have forgotten to opt for the essence.

When our secret fears come into conscious awareness, it's an opportunity for a perception correction. By recognizing we don't feel happy, we give the emotion, the *belief* to the Holy Spirit for correction. This is the right use of our will. As we let go of being "right" and welcome a different perception, our minds are healed of the belief in separation. When we perceive a problem, we can stop and ASK to *see* differently. We do not give our perceived solutions to the Holy Spirit as a list of demands. The Peace of God is Reality. By using the world as our imagined source, we are defending against our *Real* Source. When we want something *other* than the Peace of God, we'll stick peace somewhere on the bottom of our list after a new car.

> *"I want the peace of God. To say these words is nothing. But to mean these words is everything."*
> *ACIM Workbook Lesson 185*

Once, I received a letter telling me I could trade in my car for a new one and not increase my payment. Happiness appeared to come from this letter! I could get a new car! I went to the dealership to get the new car. It turns out the letter was a come-on. Anger appeared to come because of the letter! I withheld peace from myself. How dare they waste my time (actually my illusion of time)! It seemed as if something outside was taking my peace away. I was certain I needed a new car for the same payment so I could be peaceful and happy. I had given a letter, a piece of paper, meaning. This was the rule I made up about it in my mind.

I left in the same old car. There was nothing wrong with my car, only with my thoughts. Time appeared to pass. I had a car accident. A tow truck took the smashed car away. A lady from the insurance company called and declared the car "totaled." Suddenly, I appeared to love the old car. I withheld peace from myself. In a moment of upset, I judged that having my old car "totaled" meant loss. This was the meaning I had given to "totaled." Then the lady explained that they would send me a check and I would get a new car! The peace came back.

Interesting.

Peace was within me all along. I had not really wanted peace the whole time. If I had really wanted peace that whole time, I could have:

- Gotten a piece of paper in the mail
- Gone to the car dealership
- Found out the mailing was a come-on
- Left in the same old car
- Had a car accident
- Found out the car was "totaled"

- Bought a new car
- Enjoyed a consistent experience of peace the whole time

My experience of peace had been inconsistent because I was making it dependent on a car, dependent on getting "my way" in the world. *A Course in Miracles* tells us, *"Peace of mind is clearly an internal matter. 3 It must begin with your own thoughts, and then extend outward. 4 It is from your peace of mind that a peaceful perception of the world arises"* (ACIM Workbook Lesson 34).

Our individual life curriculum is perfectly constructed by our True Inner Teacher. The Perfect Plan for Universal Healing of all untrue thoughts is already underway. You are part of The Plan for the Happiness of All. *You are not controlling it.* Healing doesn't occur by altering external events. The search for externals is the ego's plan. Guess what. The ego's plan is to stay afraid and miserable. It teaches us to never, ever look at our underlying fear of God.

Fear will insist we *need* this situation, that person, then another. Oh, that didn't work? Okay, seek for something else. The ego is the voice of fear. It tells us we have betrayed God and deserve to die. If we keep it as our master, we will eventually run out of time. All forms of fear are self-imposed barriers to our awareness of Love's Presence, God's Presence. When we observe our attraction to guilt, we can make a different choice. Our willingness *is* necessary. To let go of the attraction to guilt, we must stop trying to make conditions and relationships into the source of love, joy and peace. Trying to replace God makes us very uncomfortable. We blame conditions and relationships for the discomfort. We even try to blame God. The option to *choose again* is available at any moment.

A Course in Miracles is a practical course. It works in our lives when we apply it. The Spirit of Love will re-interpret what we see upon request. Finally, we are asking for something useful—the truth. We are choosing God (Love). We are remembering the love within ourselves and everyone. Love *is everything already.* We are letting go of the block to love in our own awareness. I had a business situation that I could not resolve for a long time. The standstill showed me a block in my awareness. The situation appeared complicated. I kept seeking for a solution on the surface level and couldn't find it. Intuitively, I knew the answer had to do with Oneness, but I couldn't figure out what that looked like. The search for Oneness on the level of form was not working. Eventually, I realized I was seeing one person in the situation as guilty. *(Aha!)*

When we judge, we are having an illusion. If we are not wholly joyous, we are judging; thinking something that God would not think. Our minds are blank. But we can let go of the idea that is hurting us. It isn't real. So I let go of my perception of this person's guilt and remembered that God is in this person. I shifted my focus from the level of the problem and remembered love.

Suddenly, the solution flashed into my mind.
The answer had been there the whole time.
It was obvious.

When we let go of our belief in guilt, the solution comes shining into our awareness. *The Course* doesn't leave us dangling with our plans not working. It does NOT tell us, "Too bad; nothing you try to do within your thought system will work because you are dreaming. Deal with it." The *Course* tells us to be of cheer. All we have to do is to be willing to love. We are learning how to relax our defenses against the Plan that works and is Universally Happy. As we step back, the problems we *perceived* dissolve. Our mind is being returned to the awareness of peace. We are being shown how to remember that beyond all else, peace really is what we want. Forgetting what we really wanted was the problem. When we place our minds on peace, we are returning to the healthy thought system. Instead of attempting to make ourselves comfortable by inappropriate means, we remember the truth. We are choosing to Think with God.

> We are returning our minds to the Kingdom.
> All else is added effortlessly.

Miracles require no planning from us. Everyone's part fits together impeccably in the Universal Happiness Plan for healing. One of the funniest lines in the *Course* is, *"You who cannot even control yourselves should hardly aspire to control the universe"* (ACIM. 11.IX.11). I can't read that without laughing. Can you? It reminds me to focus on the mind training. When we judge, we fool ourselves with the untrue belief we know everything. God's Universal Happiness Plan leads us out of the hallucination of rightness. Our job is to relinquish the foolish insistence that we are in charge. How could we possibly direct a Plan when we don't know what anything is for? As we let go of judging ourselves and one another for not being able to see everything throughout space and time, our joy rises. We can receive the Higher Instructions and use our hands and feet as instruments of healing.

Lesson 71 from the Workbook of the *Course* gives us specific guidelines for accessing our instructions. Instead of the upside down way of telling God, "Here is my list for the day, now God, please bless it," we ask:

What would You have me do?
Where would You have me go?
What would You have me say, and to whom?

The lesson assures us that, *"He will answer in proportion to your willingness to hear His Voice. Refuse not to hear."*

My schedule is not the same day to day. Usually in the summer, I play concerts in an orchestra. At Christmastime, I often play holiday concerts. One spring, I got an idea. It was a self-initiated plan. It came not from Divine Guidance but from a subtle belief that I had to make my own provisions to be safe. I decided to call venues before my busy summer season and book a full Christmas season of holiday concerts. It was convenient for me and I would be sure to have a December brimming with concerts and *money*! I congratulated myself on this brilliant plan and forgot all about following God's Plan.

Despite making all the "right" earth plane moves, I could not book one concert. Feeling frustrated and stymied did not remind me of Christmas. I realized the issue was not the inability to get my way in the world. The only problem was wanting what I assumed I had to have in the world, so I dropped it. When I let the "need" go, peace blossomed in my awareness. Peace was what I really wanted.

Time passed. One day, I was practicing Lesson 164 from *A Course in Miracles*, *"Now are we one with Him Who is our Source."* I did not approach this meditation lesson with

111

any sense of anticipation. I wasn't expecting it to blow my mind. Today, that cracks me up. The ego blows off the truth. The unreal self doesn't want the truth because that is its undoing.

The ego doesn't want us to meditate. "Oh, that lesson, 'Now we are One with our Source.' Yawn! Boring! This isn't resonating…What's on TV tonight? Remember to call the sprinkler guy later today…Write a reminder…She had nerve to say that to me last week…Thirsty…Chocolate!"

The lesson had never astonished me before because I had never followed the instructions. This time I did. There was no big secret. There was no mystery to solve and nothing to figure out. All I did was sit with my eyes closed and my heart-mind open.

Lesson 164 describes the spiritual gifts available by simply following the instructions. It says we will *"see through the eyes of Christ."* We can *"exchange all of our suffering for joy"* this very day! The *"experience of Christ can be born in me,"* in you today! Here comes the sentence the ego had always defended against: *"Open the curtain in your practicing by merely letting go all things you think you want."*

(There goes the vision board!)

Before I opened my heart-mind, the ego had declared that impossible. "Yeah, right. Let go of everything I think I want." This time, I embraced it. In previous years, I was reading the words, closing my eyes and shutting my heart. **The Holy Spirit hears our hearts.** Our willingness is necessary. This time, I noticed the word "think." I'm not being asked to sacrifice. I am not letting go of what I *really* want, only what I *think* I want. That one word helped me so much.

I became willing and set about practicing. That practice and I are now in love. Now I practice letting go of "not-wanting" too. When I emphatically *"don't want"* something, that is also a secret "want." It is telling, not asking. "Anything-but-that-God" is fear, resistance to a condition. Resistance is affirmation. When we fear something, we are calling it to us—attracting. We're placing our mind on it and adding some emotion to go along. If you swear you will never-ever-ever have a cat or befriend a clown, you can hear the faint sound of a meow and a squeaky nose in your future. (You are giving yourself the opportunity to open to love.)

Next, I noticed that my "wants" and "don't-wants" all have something to do with me as a small, separate self. They have nothing to do with the Christ Self that God Created. As I release my attachments, I find my true heart's desire—the experience of Christ. We are all free. We can block the experience of Christ Consciousness by wishing for something else, but Our Christ Self is not *conditionally* Joyful. Our Christ Self is not dependent on something outside changing or not changing. In Reality, we are of God.

We are the Essence.

"Truth is restored to you through your desire, as it was lost to you through your desire for something else. Open the holy place which you closed off by valuing the 'something else,' and what was never lost will quietly return. It has been saved for you."

ACIM.20.IX.67

At the beginning of the spiritual path, we find out we have a Higher Self, a Christ Consciousness. It's such exciting news.

I have a Higher Self! Everyone has a Higher Self! Hallelujah! Next, we consider listening to the Higher Self. Then we actually follow the Divine Guidance with increasing consistency. This is the path to identifying with the Christ Mind. Trust is identification. We are learning to live as Our Christ Self.

We are realizing the small self was never real. God didn't create small selves. Our small self is not becoming divine. (God did not create billions of small selves that would figure out how to get their little separate ways in the world in order to be happy.) Our Higher Self is the Self God Created. We are letting go of identifying with our small self because we are trusting more and more in God and the Self God created. Through practice we develop trust.

By dropping my habitual "wants" and "not-wants," I was letting go of identifying with my unreal self. I am using the power of my mind to choose the experience of the Christ Self. This choice is gifting me with more glimpses of Oneness. It had become clear the outside world was not responsible for my happiness. I was ready to find another way. The practice of surrender was meaningless until I brought willingness. If you are not willing yet, that's okay. Tuck this away. Maybe one day there will be something you imagine you need. If that causes you any discomfort, or if you can't stand it anymore, consider this practice. Consider that the problem is not the world. You don't have to try harder, wait longer, or fix yourself. You could let go of what you think you want. Allow space for present happiness.

Your Christ Mind is joyful now. No matter what seems to happen in your life, your Christ Mind is not suffering. The Self that God created is happy as a clam. You are free to present a case for misery if you want because you are free. The Christ that is your Real Self is Eternally Joyful.

"Unless I look upon what is not there, my present happiness is all I see."

ACIM Workbook Lesson 291

After the summer, my phone started to ring. Venues called and invited me to play Christmas concerts. I performed exactly where I was intended to play and met the people I was supposed to encounter according to God's Plan. Everyone we are to meet will find us. The Holy Spirit makes the assignments. When we remember that God is the Source of our love, peace and joy, we can't lose. When we're not looking to get our peace, love and joy from other people, from situations, we remain stable. We extend peace and joy to the people who are sent to us. By giving peace and joy, we remember we have an unlimited supply. We are not entering situations or relationships trying to "get." We enter as our Christ Self. Joy is free to shine through us into the situation. We have freed the situation, the relationship, from our imaginary needs.

"Your passage through time and space is not random. You cannot but be in the right place at the right time. Such is the strength of God."

ACIM Workbook Lesson 42

PRACTICE:

In this moment, I accept my part.

I release the world and everyone in it from what I imagined I needed them and it to do for me.

Now, I allow my True Source to shine into my awareness, my mind, heart, and energy field.

And now I see the light of Truth shine through, blessing the world and everyone in it.

We all share this same Source.

With gratitude, I allow this Presence into my awareness.

I welcome Divine Joy into every encounter, into every situation, into every relationship.

By desiring Only the Presence of Truth, I am bringing the Gift of Peace to the world.

I am extending Joy to the world.

Love is extending to the world through and as me now.

In my mind's eye, I see the impact of my willingness.

This is my gift to everyone including my Self.

My supply is infinite because my Source is Infinite.

And so it is.

Amen.

By extending love to those who are sent to us, our awareness of our Source grows in our minds. We are teaching by demonstration that God is here, within us. We have enough to share because our Source is unlimited. If we forget, we remember more quickly because we value the Joy of God so much. Each encounter is an opportunity to remember Who We Are by remembering Who the other person is to us.

Today, I am still practicing breaking the lack-habit I taught myself. I don't blame the world, society, or anyone for the habits I taught myself. If I did, I would consciously break the blame habit. Our minds are so powerful because of Who Created us. From the time we were children, we began letting go of habits that no longer served us. We can do it when we let our Higher Self lead the way.

When I forget, my emotions immediately remind me of my intention. God has already given me everything of value. The joy we share with God has nothing to do with the shallow, temporary happiness of getting our way in the world. It's the depth of experiencing the truth of our relationship with our Creator. It's indescribable. But we can experience it when we let go of trying to substitute for it.

Surrender is releasing fear of truth.

Before the first experience, we call upon our faith in order to make the leap. We can recognize that the habit of external seeking is not fulfilling us. We can give our trust to these practices. Fruit will come. One day, I sat down with my lesson, and joy and gratitude filled my heart. The Lessons work. All we have to do is follow the instructions, apply them to our lives and receive the gifts. The Holy Spirit brings the healing. Our part is simple.

By letting go of "wanting," we free situations and relationships from our false sense of need. We are no longer going into the world to get. "Want" has always been an illusion because there is no lack in God.

The Joy of God is not like anything we could get from a situation or from someone else. Because it's always here, it can't be lost. The Joy of God is unconditional. God does not deprive us of Joy for any reason. It's right here when we turn to it because we can't leave our Source. God has never left us. We learn through practice that the experience of the Presence of God is what we value. Our demonstration is a gift to everyone we encounter because they are a part of us. By bringing the Joy of God, we are extending it, growing it. God is always extending because Love extends.

Part of our mind remembers that what we've really wanted all along is to live as our Christ Self. As we experience the moments of living as our Christ Self, then any time we forget, we get back on track quickly.

Nothing can compare to the Self that God Created by extension.

LOOK AT YOUR SECRET FEARS

CHOCOLATE, BATS AND CONTROL

Once, I travelled to Costa Rica with my brother. We spent several days at a yoga retreat, nestled in a remote area of the secondary rainforest. A primary rainforest is untouched by logging or human interference. It exists in its natural state. The secondary rainforest has regrown and exudes the energy of resurrection, similar to the energy transmitted in reiki treatments. When my brother and I arrived at the retreat center in the Central Mountain Region of the secondary rainforest, our friendly hosts greeted us with fresh fruit smoothies. We immediately relaxed and tuned in to the slower pace and high vibrational frequencies.

Each morning, we enjoyed yoga classes in an open-air studio that overlooked the lush canopies of forest. We marveled at the colorful toucans and scarlet macaws. Short, powerful bursts of rain brought the scents of earth and flowers to life each afternoon. We enjoyed fresh organic meals served on a balcony that jutted out over the forest. At night, the sounds of wildlife surrounded the casitas and sang us to sleep. One day, we visited a coffee plantation. The coffee farmer took us on a tour of the plantation and showed us how the beans were grown and processed. My brother spoke enough Spanish to translate for me. We dipped our hands into vats of rich coffee beans and breathed in their aroma.

The farmer guided us on a vigorous hike up a large creek. We stopped to see a small cave, which he explained was a bat cave! He warned us not to inhale when we poked our heads in the cave, as the bat droppings might contain a fungus that could cause lung disease. I was not interested in putting my head in a bat cave, anyway.

As the hike continued, the creek became deeper, and the water ran faster. We were hiking to a waterfall. I slowed my pace as I became intentional with each step and placed my feet on the slippery rocks one foot at a time. The farmer became impatient with this plodding tourist who did not even want to see bats. When we arrived at the majestic waterfall, the energy shifted. We were all spellbound. Time slowed down. I spontaneously played a melody on the small ocarina I had been wearing on a string around my neck. A sweet song of thanks to the waterfall blew through my lips and the ocarina. The oneness of all life was palpable. A large blue morpho butterfly flew by in what seemed to be slow motion. We all loved one another again. It occurred to my brother to ask the farmer if the waterfall had a name. The farmer said, "The Hope of the Vampire Bat." (He said this in Spanish.) We hiked downstream in harmony and wonder. The farmer fed us a delicious meal of foods cultivated on his land. Our hosts retrieved us and brought us back to the retreat center.

Next, we decided to go to the Cloud Forest in Monteverde. The higher elevation of Cloud Forests brings the earth to meet the clouds. Monteverde was more developed for ecotourism. There were biologists available for guided tours of the forest. Ecotourists, ecologists and wildlife coexist in a cool mist. After checking in at our green hotel, we asked around about interesting things to do there. Someone suggested the Bat Museum and Chocolate Shop. They had me at "Chocolate Shop." We intended to go to the chocolate part first. When we arrived, we saw a sign that said, "Bat Feeding 3:00." Since it was exactly three in the afternoon, we headed into the Bat Museum (suspecting nothing). An interesting biologist told us all about bats before we watched the feeding. I fell in love with bats that day! The bat-loving biologist asked us, "How many of you came here for the chocolate?" We all raised our hands. He said, "We do that on purpose. It's hard to get people in the doors for bats."

If I had called this chapter "Control, Bats and Shame," would you have read it? (Maybe yes; maybe no.) Shame is trending these days. Soon shame will have its own national holiday with a parade and greeting cards.

The new thing about shame is the way we look at it.

Just like bats.

Now we actually *consider* addressing shame. When we look at shame with the Holy Spirit, we discover it isn't real. If we *hide* it, we go around believing stuff that isn't true. If I hadn't gone to the Bat Museum, I would still trust the bad press about bats. Learning the Truth dispelled my fear thoughts about these truly helpful flying mammals. My willingness to let go of judgment against bats and learn the Truth bore fruit. Did you realize that bats keep the mosquito populations low? This is just *one* of the many wonderful facts I learned when I was willing to face my fears and enter the bat cave. Before that day, I did not know the Truth. I hardly ever contemplated bats. That's how it was with shame too.

I hardly ever considered it. But the *results* of my hidden shame thoughts showed.

There seemed to be a steady stream of controlling, critical people in my life. *How dare they!* Nothing I did was good enough (for these people, I told myself). No matter how much I achieved, no matter how hard I tried, (*they*) told me I was not good enough. (They) tried to change me. I really did not like (controlling people). I really did not like (critical people).

It occurred to me that I used to act the same way.

When I acted that way, I was not aware of my behavior. I trusted my "good intentions," my little strength. (Ego) I was sure *my* plan was best for everyone. (I wasn't asking. I was telling.) One day, two controlling, critical, enthusiastic, well-intentioned people showed up in two completely different aspects of my life at the same time. They had plans to fix the organizations! They wanted to make them better "for the benefit of all involved," they told us! (They were not managers or anything like that, just enthusiastic people telling everyone what to do.) Both well-functioning, not-needing-to-be-fixed groups of people started to become miserable. Neither group of people responded well to its unasked-for makeover.

Everyone forgot to laugh.

I noticed this happening in two aspects of my life at the same time. Clearly, this behavior was not fun-inducing. Both people were *Self-Forgiveness-Opportunity-Delivery-People!* I dropped *my* not-fun-inducing behavior. Both organizations returned to normal. People started laughing again. People closer to home started laughing too.

The experience taught me the difference between "helping" and being Truly Helpful. Following the Guidance of the Holy Spirit is Truly Helpful. The ego's made-up plans lead to "helping" the ego. Bats are Truly Helpful. They are humble (and have terrible publicists). They have no interest in feeding the ego. Vampire bats *don't* suck. They lick. An anticoagulant contained in their saliva may soon be used to treat human heart conditions and the effects of strokes. When I am listening to my ego (judging), I think I know everything. I don't. Without the Holy Spirit, my "helping" doesn't accomplish spit.

Time appeared to pass. Shadow (stick) figures still showed up in my life with this behavior. "Aha!" I told myself. "I know what to do! Even though I have dropped the *behavior*, I forgot to *forgive* myself for it. *SHAZAM*—I forgive me. Yeah! I *love* my *new* Self-Forgiveness-Opportunity-Delivery-People."

And they kept on coming.
"Really?!"

I looked at my behavior to be sure I wasn't still accidentally doing it. I gave my willingness to the Holy Spirit; supercalifragilisticexpialidocious-willingness. "Fixing" myself would not work. "Fixing" was *showing up* as the problem. It was not the answer. "Please Holy Spirit, send the answer." Next, a wonderful thing happened:

Someone shamed me.

It was a vicious, unprovoked, out of the blue *shaming*. I was sitting there reading. *Wheel of Fortune* spun on the television. This brother (then boyfriend) woke out of a nap and started in on me, going right to my Core Innocence (saying I'm not). My mind flashed on this quote from the *Course*, *"When you feel the holiness of your relationship is threatened by anything, stop instantly and offer the Holy Spirit (your willingness in spite of fear to let Him exchange this instant for the holy one which you would rather have)"* (ACIM 18.VI.46). The quote was right there on the tip of my brain and came directly into my mind. I started very slowly (inside my head) repeating, "Holy Spirit... Holy Spirit... Holy Spirit... Holy Spirit... Holy Spirit..."

Suddenly (mid-shaming), I became filled with light and peace and joy. Oxygen came from my lungs and words came out of my mouth. My personal self stepped to the side. "Pamela" watched in amazement as the Holy Spirit broke up with this brother (calmly, firmly and completely). "Pamela" was overjoyed and astonished that she had invoked the Holy Spirit. "She" didn't mind at all about a breakup. "Pamela" also heard, "She could be worried, but she isn't." (Don't ask me who said that. I don't know.)

Wow!

In that moment, my mind was healed of an old fear thought I hadn't even known was there. I no longer believed my happiness depended on being in a romantic relationship. Emotional dependence disappeared! The man moved out. Joy moved into Awareness. I danced around the house. The dog became my dance partner. We both enjoyed this immensely. I broke into loud-don't-care-if-it's-in-tune song at regular intervals, just for fun. I also heard from within, "Happiness is not dependent on *not* being in a relationship either." (Oh right, the flip side.)

Not much time appeared to pass. Strong Holy Guidance led me into another situation (not related to romance). A boat captain invited me to teach *A Course in Miracles* on his boat. Some born again Christians arrived on the scene and became my saviors. They bestowed upon me another shaming. I was "Adam-and-Eved"! It sliced through my emotional body. *Yuck!* On the *intellectual level,* I do not see women as sinful. I am a New Thought Woman! Women can talk about God! Sin is not real (said my brain)! During the Garden Style Dress Down, I kept checking within and asking for directions. Very Clear Thoughts told me, "Don't judge back, and don't judge the situation." But I *felt* as if I was being given surgery without anesthesia (and not the John of God from Brazil kind). I was having a shame-*ectomy.*

Finally.
It had a name.

Nobody even said the *word* in these situations. I just *knew* it. Shame no longer hid in the dark attracting pointy sticks and stones. I had asked for the answer while the problem was still unclear. The problem had been a secret I kept hidden from myself. The Holy Spirit sent a team of saviors to show me the problem thought so I could recognize it and let it go to the light.

> *"A problem cannot be solved if you do not know what it is. Even if it is really solved already, you will still have the problem because you cannot recognize that it has been solved. This is the situation of the world. The problem of separation, which is really the only problem, has already been solved. But the solution is not recognized because the problem is not recognized." Workbook Lesson 79*

I found out a lot about shame after that. I learned that shame, control and criticism hang out together. So many saviors had come to set me free. Plenty of subconscious shame-carriers had been attracted to and by me. We were all given the opportunity to see shame as NOTHING together. The root of the word "shame" means "to cover." Oh you, upper subconscious level! You veil over the True Self!

Shames goes beyond feeling guilty about *doing something* in the world. I did not feel guilty about sitting on the bed reading. I did not feel guilty about teaching *A Course in Miracles* or saying yes to a situation to which I had been profoundly led, step by step, by my Inner Holy Guidance. This was about my relationship with me, My Self and I. It was time to look at how I *really* felt about My Relationship with God.

Shame is the cover we put over our True Identity.

It's our in-security blanket.

Our True Identity is Innocent (and doesn't need a blanky).

Shame (like all not-God thoughts) projects. It's a block to the awareness of Love's Eternal Presence. The time had come to look *honestly* at how I felt about *being in the world*. Sitting alone on the bed, I asked. With profound willingness, I asked with open ears. There was no TV, no dog, no dancing and singing. There was me sitting still, willing to see my Self as God created me. I asked for the belief in shame to be lifted off my Holy, God Created Mind.

I admitted that I:

1. Was scared.
2. Couldn't do it myself.
3. Didn't comprehend what I was supposed to do.

But I went for it, anyway.

Sensing sleep closing in, I gave my sleep to the Holy Spirit. That night, I had a gentle dream. In the morning, I clearly remembered the symbols in the dream. My earthly father's name appeared in the dream. The word "share" also surfaced in the dream. At the time, I was not speaking to my earthly father. For years, I believed the pain in the relationship was coming from his alcoholism and abuse. I had not yet accepted that I am only at the affect of *my* choice to withhold Love from my own awareness. The *Course* had told me the Truth on every page. But I had made someone *else* responsible for how I felt about myself. Now I was *willing* to heal.

Opening the *Course* to my morning Workbook lesson, I saw my instructions. I was being asked to forgive a brother this morning. The lesson asked me to call to mind an "enemy." Oh Holy Spirit, You are So Smart! You *Knew* today's lesson *last night!* That's why the Holy Spirit is in charge of the Universal Happiness Plan. We aren't because we don't understand what to do. We *accept* our part in the Plan by being willing.

The lesson for the day gave specific instructions to call a brother to mind and *share* peace and joy with them. The *Course* was perfectly clear. My earthly father was not the problem. I had denied peace and joy to this equal Son of God. I had perceived him as an enemy and withheld the awareness of peace and joy from my own Self. By seeing him as an Equal Son of God (not a body) and by offering him peace and joy, I got to *receive* peace and joy. I received the awareness that we were both Sons of God. By giving Truth, I received Truth. By seeing that only the Love is Real about my earthly father, I got to experience that only the Love is Real about me too!

I *experienced* my earthly father as my savior.

(Cue the chorus!)

Hallelujah!

> *"True giving is creation. It extends the limitless to the unlimited, eternity to timelessness, and love unto itself. It adds to all that is complete already, not in simple terms of adding more, for that implies that it was less before. It adds by letting what cannot contain itself fulfill its aim of giving everything it has away, securing it forever for itself."*
>
> *ACIM Workbook Lesson 105*

Love created us by extending. God gave Bill Maher to the world by extending Love. God gave Bill Maher to us. Bill Maher is the extension of The Love of God. That's right. Bill Maher is God's gift to the world! So are You, so am I. *And so is the person flashing through your mind right now.*

We are all equal extensions (gifts) of the Love of God to the Love of God. Our acceptance of Love does not make it True. Belief (Faith) has everything to do with whether we continue to extend, or whether we hide the Truth from ourselves and one another. When we cover the Truth, we are still Extensions of God. We are still the Peace of God, the Love of God, the Joy of God.

Bats still keep the mosquito population down even if many people don't know that. Bats are still wonderful even when some people are fooled by the vampire-Hollywood misperceptions. The Truth about bats has never changed. God did not lose anything by giving us Bill Maher. God did not lose anything by giving us bats. God did not lose anything by giving us YOU. Being Love, God can never lose and extends forever. Bill Maher is an *extension* of God. God is in Bill Maher (because God is in my mind). God is in bats (because God is in my mind).

Okay. I'll wait for you to be done. Very funny.
Take a breath.

YOU are an *extension* of God. God is in YOU (because God is in my mind and *yours*). We are all Thoughts in God's Infinite Mind. The *Course* tells us, *"The word 'sin' should be changed to 'lack of love' because 'sin' is a man-made word with threat connotations which he made up himself. No real threat is involved anywhere. Nothing is gained by frightening yourselves, and it is very destructive to do so."* (1.1 Miracle Principle 25)

We think we separated from God because we are walking around (or sitting around or dancing around) in bodies. Because we are here, we think we have sinned. We might not even believe the whole Adam and Eve sin-sin-sinny story intellectually. But our subconscious fear about our relationship with God shows. That *does not mean* the fear is justified. It shows up so we can *recognize it is meaningless*. We face it with the Holy Spirit so we can accept the nothingness and heal.

"My brother, you are part of God and part of me. When you have at last looked at the ego's foundation without

shrinking, you will also have looked upon ours. I come to
you from our Father to offer you everything again. Do not
refuse it in order to keep a dark cornerstone hidden, for its
protection will not save you. I give you the lamp and I will
go with you. You will not take this journey alone. I will lead
*you to your **true** Father, Who hath need of you as I have.*
Will you not answer the call of love with joy?"

ACIM.10.3.4

We are released from the shame of separation by seeing that it is *not real.* Our relationships give us this Divine
opportunity. Separation was a wrong perception, not a
"sin" at all. The Love has always been. We open our minds
to see the Truth, to *feel* it. God (Love) did not lose us. We
did not do anything to God (Love). There is no lack of
Love. God is not mad at us. We are now and always have
been perfectly created extensions of Divine Love. This
is the Equal Truth about Everyone. Truth is unequivocal
and *has* to apply to Everyone. Our "not-God" (unloving)
thoughts are nothing. When we give our meaningless
thought forms to the Light, we see the equal extensions
of love in all life. By extending this True Thought, love
is restored to *our* Awareness. We recognize the light that
always has been.

"Enlightenment is but a recognition, not a change at all."
ACIM Workbook Lesson 188

God bless you shame-bearing people. Literally, bless
you. I see you as clean and free. May the Peace and Joy and
Love of God shine from my heart-mind to yours. I experience myself as free, loving, peaceful and joyous by seeing

the Truth in you. Eternal Innocence Created us infinitely loved and loving. We hung out in the darkness for eons when we viewed the world from an upside perspective. In Truth, we have been the Son of God all along. Now we will use our highly evolved sense of hearing to follow the Voice of God. The fruit was good, but thank Heavens we can give up eating those bugs! Now we can fly in the light of our True Nature, our True Environment.

(I hear the chocolate is excellent.)

SAY GOODBYE TO SPECIALNESS

I SEE INNOCENT PEOPLE

A Course in Miracles says, *"Forgiveness is the end of specialness"* (ACIM.24.IV.26). Seems important, huh? But why would forgiveness end specialness? Isn't specialness a good thing? Am I not the apple of God's Divine Eye? The Real (Christ) Self is the shared, Holy Love of God and is Eternally joined with God and all of Creation. The *Course* uses the word specialness to describe our illusion of separateness and superiority. This small self, the hero of its own storyline, set apart from the rest of Creation and its Creator has a backstory.

> Grab and comfy blanket and a cup of tea.
> Open to learning new ideas about time.

Once upon a time, there was no time, only Eternity. We told our Creator a joke, "God, give me all the Love. Just me, not them." We forgot this was a joke. The *Course* says we forgot to laugh. Being the Divine Intelligence of the Universe, God said "no" to this "tiny, mad idea." The Love of God is shared. We could not divide it. Then, the first tantrum was born. "Uh-huh! I'll show you, God! I will make an entire world where I *will* be special. *And* I will go forth and seek special love in this made-up world. In this world, I will

seek special love outside of me in relationships and situations. Perhaps I will try to find it in things or behaviors."
Some names for specialness were "idolatry," "dependency"
or "codependence." It could show up as an attachment to
outcome.

Many times, specialness hid in our upper subconscious
level, driving decisions and behaviors. (See Stick Figure 2.)
It appeared as obsessive thoughts that blocked our minds
from experiencing ever-present joy, love and peace. We
could engage in our favorite activities and still not enjoy
them. Thoughts of the past or worries about the future pre-
occupied our minds. Without letting go of the illusion of
specialness, we could not experience the present Presence
of Joy, Peace and Love that is our Eternal Truth.

Specialness was a defense against God. We used thoughts
about the past and future to block the Eternal Presence of
God from our awareness. We were trying to be right and
make God wrong. No matter what it looked like, specialness was always fear. Trying to prove God wrong was a lot of
pressure. It took great effort to pretend to be a separate self.
We did not know why we felt separate from our Source. We
forgot we were choosing to replace the unlimited, shared
Love of God with an illusion of specialness.

> "Time and eternity cannot both be real, because they con-
> tradict each other."
>
> *ACIM 9.XI.107*

Like all illusions, specialness had a limited shelf life.
When we tried to use people or situations to replace God
as our Source, we felt guilty. Part of our minds knew what
we were doing. We were trying to defy God. Guilt felt

uncomfortable, so we tried to project it onto the "special" people and situations. "Look, God! *They* are doing it. Not me! I am innocent! (I am better than *them* and still trying to be special!)" But whenever we tried to project guilt, it only made us feel worse. Sometimes the fear would arise when a "special" something or someone would go away. "Oh no! I think I have to have that to be happy (because I am using it as a replacement for my Source!)"

In our made-up world of specialness, we viewed ourselves as we wanted to be seen, even if it was in a derogatory light. We saw our own projected thoughts about our "selves." The "selves" in the made-up world didn't know they weren't really separate. They believed they were bodies that died and had to pay taxes. They didn't recognize each other and only saw their illusions. The made-up "special" selves didn't recognize the Real Self that God Created.

God had said "no," so this made up-world was not real. It only *seemed* real. When we forgot to laugh, God's endless Love immediately extended the Holy Spirit to us. The Holy Spirit was God's Answer. Through the Holy Spirit, we were able to come back to our Right Mind in God and recognize we were only dreaming. It all happened in a flash—the tiny, mad idea, God's Answer (Holy Spirit) and resistance to God's Answer (which was called the ego). Because we could never *really* separate, the whole misadventure had been nothing but a series of flashbacks we have been remembering while safe at Home in the Mind of God. We are Thoughts in God's Mind. God's Mind has not changed. God is still Eternal Love.

Even in what appears to be now, in what seems to be time and space, while you or I have life events and then give them to the Holy Spirit to be forgiven, we are remembering.

Time is not happening the way we imagine it because our True Self is Eternal. We wake up to the Truth by forgiving ourselves and we forgive ourselves by forgiving others. This is the perfect system that appears to be healing us now, but really already happened. Because of Who We Really Are, our only Real Relationship (Creator and Created) is intact. Specialness was just a joke without a punchline. It never happened! We have never been bodies with egos. We have always been the One Self that God Created.

By giving our willingness to have our belief in specialness undone, our "special relationships" are revealed to us to be made Holy. Because we are all in One Eternal Holy Creation and Creator Relationship, our True Relationship is Healthy and Happy. We are Spirit and live in a state of Eternal Grace. In the dream, our minds are healed by inviting the Holy Spirit into our relationships. It is the destiny of all of our relationships to shift from "special" to Holy. Since situations are relationships too, all of our "special situations" are destined to heal by shifting into their natural state of Holiness. Once we invite the Holy Spirit into our relationships, Holiness gets to work right away! Sometimes it seems as if we are being turned upside down. In Reality, our relationships are being sorted out and turned right side up. The *purpose* is shifting from fear to Love.

The Course advises us that *"this is the time for faith"* (ACIM 17.VI.48). When we give a relationship to the Holy Spirit, we are also surrendering the *form* of the relationship. Maybe the form will stay the same. Maybe it will change. The relationship is being dedicated to the Highest Good. That Highest Good is not separate. Our good is shared. We are learning that our will is the same as God's Will. We are learning that our minds are One.

Once, the Holy Spirit led me into a romantic relationship. I immediately gave the relationship to the Holy Spirit for Christ's purposes. At the start of the relationship, the man told me that if we ever broke up, we would never meet again. He was adamant about this. Lessons arose rapidly, and I continually gave my false perceptions to the Holy Spirit to be undone. I understood why this man and I had been assigned to one another. The romantic form was fertile ground for untrue thoughts to surface for forgiveness. I gave over each illusion that arose. One day, the man looked me in the eyes and told me I was unlovable. My heart filled with joy and I exclaimed, "Thank you!" This shocked both of us. It seemed inappropriate! But in that moment I knew that:

1. The man was projecting an illusion about himself onto me.
2. It wasn't true about him or about me.
3. We were both healed in the same instant.
4. Our minds were joined.

The next day, the man was kissing my hands and calling me a saint. It was a miracle. We had seen the Christ in each other. It seemed as if our work had completed. I thanked the Holy Spirit and asked if there was any more healing work for us to do. I heard, "Now you will change the form of the relationship, while knowing that change of form does not mean guilt. *Nothing* means guilt." As soon as I heard the communication in my heart, I knew it was True. The man and I prayed about this change of form and gave our faith to the prayer. We experienced a seamless shift in form to a loving brother-sister bond of steadfast friendship. The previous form had served its function. I recognized the lesson was universally applicable.

Nothing means guilt.

My now devoted brother told me, "You are ready to reconcile with your father." It was true. I had accepted my innocence and lovability and could move beyond *forgiveness-as-long-as-we-don't-speak.* As I picked up the telephone, I surrendered the conversation to the Holy Spirit. Pray, pray, pray... ring, ring, ring... There was no answer and no voicemail. The next day, I tried again. Holy Spirit, Holy Spirit, Holy Spirit... Pray, pray, pray... ring, ring, ring... This went on for several days. One day, as the phone rang, I started to pray, and the thought came, "This is not a big deal." Peace came over me. The "specialness" had disappeared. The illusion of specialness had been the problem. My next thought was, "Now the call will go through." And it did. Our relationship healed. He didn't change. I had learned to love myself. On the day he died, I knew everything was healed. The feeling came over me that we had accomplished our forgiveness work together. I found out about an hour later that he had passed.

Now when I think of him I am filled with joy and gratitude that we completed our assignment. He is a benign character in my mind and in my dreams. When we forgive, the problem disappears. For decades, I struggled over that special relationship. Today, I almost forgot to include him in a book about forgiveness. I asked the Holy Spirit, "What else do you want in this book?" I laughed with deep gratitude that I had forgotten I ever thought there was a problem in that relationship. Now a situation that used to bring tears brings laughter.

> *"Where darkness was I look upon the light."*
> *ACIM Lesson 302*

Because we have never separated from one another, or from God, guilt is an illusion. No one has ever succeeded in bringing separation into love. We are still as God created us because what God Created is changeless. The Holy Spirit removes the illusions of guilt and fear from our minds with our willingness. Everyone we meet is an assignment. Our assignment is always the same—allow the relationship translation from the illusion of specialness to its natural state of Holiness. This is how we forgive ourselves for what never happened. It is a collaborative process. We don't have to wait to invite the Holy Spirit into our relationships. Whenever we pick up the telephone or walk out the door, we can call the Holy Spirit into our conversations, our meetings and our thoughts.

"When you meet anyone, remember it is a holy encounter. As you see him, you will see yourself. As you treat him, you will treat yourself. As you think of him, you will think of yourself. Never forget this, for in him you will find yourself or lose sight of yourself."

ACIM.8.IV.19

PRACTICE:

We open our heart-minds and energy fields wide to the Holy Spirit, the Holy Presence of Love we all share.

Everyone who will ever read this book shares this Holy Presence with us and with one another.

We share this Holy Presence with everyone we will encounter throughout this day, with everyone who crosses our minds.

We share this Holy Presence with all of Creation and with our Creator.

This Holy Presence is a Spirit of Wholeness, and we open to the experience of our wholeness.

If there is anyone in all of creation who we have held to the side from the experience of Oneness, we choose differently in this moment.

Now we offer the willingness to recognize the Love of God we share.

This is the Truth of our Relationship.

With honesty, we recognize we can't judge. It is impossible for us to judge any situation in which we find ourselves with this person.

Our physical senses cannot perceive the entire situation.

We are not a body and they are not a body.

The Wholeness of the One Self is completely intact and we offer gratitude.

No untrue thought has ever changed what God created because nothing can change God's Creation.

The power of the Love of God is Infinite, Eternal, Boundless.

Herein lies our Innocence.

Herein lies our True Self.

We give our willingness to allow the experience of God's Love for us to rise in our awareness.

We welcome it.

And we give our willingness to feel the Love we have for all of Creation including anyone we brought into this meditation.

The Love of God is all-inclusive.

This is what we really want, more than any external circumstance in any situation.

Our Will and God's Will are One—Changeless, Infinite Eternal Love.

Thanks be to God.

Amen

Letting go of specialness is like relinquishing judgment; we realize we never had it. To forgive, we admit that we don't know everything and we aren't special. There is no loss in finding we aren't special. When the illusion of specialness falls away, we discover our Holiness—our Wholeness!

We start to regard patience differently. *A Course in Miracles* tells us, *"Patience is natural to those who trust. Sure of the ultimate interpretation of all things in time, no outcome already seen or yet to come can cause them fear"* (ACIM.M.4.20). If I am judging or making something special, I am causing myself fear. The situation isn't doing anything to me. Nothing can hurt the Self God Created. Even if I do not understand why something is happening in the dream, I can remember that I can't judge, and my good cannot be taken from me. God is my Source. I don't have to figure anything out. I don't have to wait to be joyful. Patience has nothing to do with waiting for something to change or not change in the world. It's about trusting that I will eventually receive the Holy Spirit's interpretation. All is well because that's the Holy Spirit's perception. Sometimes a situation looks really weird. But I trust that the Holy Spirit is not condemning it or anyone in it. When I admit I don't know what it means, I am being honest. By being willing to share the Holy Spirit's perception, I am surrendering to God's Will. I can't force my understanding, but I can make space in my heart-mind for God's Answer to come.

Christ is Eternal. In Reality, everyone has always been Christ. God has always been our Source. The past didn't happen the way I remember it. When I was seeing through the eyes of fear, illusions were distorting my sight. Each step in the dream has been planned for me. I have the opportunity to recognize the Truth in each moment. By relying on the Holy Spirit to meet our needs in what appears to be time, we are learning to place our faith in God's Voice. Our training is reminding us we want God's Will. This leads us to remember that we *are* God's Will. We are the Self that God Created.

By remembering that God's Will is the only Will, I view the past differently. The past was perfect, all along. There was nothing to forgive. When guitarists left WorldColor and a promoter told untruths about the band, they were paving the way for my adventure in Nepal. My trust increased. The man on the train and the police who tossed Gandhi onto the street were leading Gandhi to his enduring peace platform. The Artist Formerly Known as Mao taught me about forgiveness and showed me what needed to heal in my mind. A cat, a clown and a bug dancer opened my heart. My friend's fear of dogs reminded me to receive the present Presence of Love. My childhood church, my earthly father and a boyfriend showed me what I secretly believed about myself so my mind could be healed. Everyone I encountered had been Christ all along! I AM surrounded by the Love of God!

I see Christ people!

Glimpses of Revelation or Holy Instants remind us of the Truth because they are breakthrough moments. We can have breakthroughs without having a mystical experience because True Forgiveness shows us Who We Are. Through True Forgiveness, we find out nothing happened. No one has hurt us and we have hurt no one. Our Oneness is intact. Innocence is revealed. When we start to study *A Course in Miracles*, we read that *"forgiveness recognizes what you thought your brother did to you has not occurred"* (Workbook 2. WF.1). It sounds weird. But God said "no" to specialness because it is impossible to bring separation into Love. Shared Love is God's Will. Therefore, it is Our Will Too. We only *"thought"* we wanted specialness. Anything we thought we wanted at the expense of the joy and peace within has been an attempt at specialness. "I'll be happy when..."

When we take our mind off of form and place it on the content of joy, peace and love, we find what we *really* want. We have it already because joy, peace and love are Eternal. Making happiness dependent on the world was the way we blocked the Truth from our own experience. The world can have no effect on us when we aren't trying to it use it to replace God. And as our mind is returned to God (Atonement), we see all of our perceived problems disappear. They were illusions of unforgiveness projected from a mind that mistakenly believed it had separated.

Thank God we were only joking.

Our True Self is laughing Joyfully ever after.

"The sight of Christ is all there is to see. The song of Christ is all there is to hear. The hand of Christ is all there is to hold. There is no journey but to walk with Him."
                                                    ACIM 24.VI.46

ENCOUNTER YOUR TRUE SELF

THE NAMASTE EXPERIENCE

One New Year's Eve, I abandoned my annual resolution to drink more water. I tried something practical for a change. My resolution was to behold Christ in everyone. It was likely I would forget many times, so I included myself in the resolution. I wouldn't even need water to carry out this resolution. Whenever I remembered, I could offer my willingness. I was not imagining each person as the man Jesus, but as the light beyond their bodies. I didn't have to understand exactly what I was doing because my personality was not in charge. *A Course in Miracles* asks us if we are willing to see our brothers as sinless. That's it; just be willing. Everyone in Nepal says, "Namaste" instead of "hello" or "goodbye." "I bow to you." "The Divine Light in me recognizes the Divine Light in you." When I lived in Kathmandu, I enjoyed saying, "Namaste" frequently. Now it was time to *mean* it, to offer silent blessings throughout the day.

Formerly mundane tasks took on a whole new light. The light had been there all along; my attention had been elsewhere. Trips to the grocery store became an opportunity to experience Christ. There was no strain involved. It's easy to put food items in a cart and gently remember the Truth about people as they walk by. Without warning, my heart would fill with profound, limitless love for someone. My *Being* recognized them completely. It felt like falling in love, but without the romantic form attached to it. Sometimes I would look into someone's eyes and my heart would leap as the veil of illusion dropped.

I practiced while waiting in lines, driving in traffic and with people in my life. Sometimes I encountered active resistance to seeing Christ in people. A hidden defense would arise. My willingness was pushing up my hidden fears to be undone by the Holy Spirit. I noticed the resistance, gave it over, and restated my intention. While driving anywhere, I prayed, "Let this be a Christ to Christ encounter." These are still my practices, but I am recounting my early experiences with the practice. Once you start, you won't want to stop!

At yoga classes, the teacher would ask us to think about our intention for the class. ("Let me see Christ in everyone here.") The yoga classes were held at a gym. There were mirrors on the walls so I let my eyes rest on each person during the class and give my willingness to recognize the Christ in them. One day, I had been practicing throughout the class and was doing a downward dog pose. The teacher approached me from the front and gave me an instruction to adjust my foot. When she said my name, I looked up into her eyes.

Bam!!

This time I felt the shared limitless Love of God while still being aware of my body. It was like the direct encounter with God, but I did not leave time and space. Part of my mind was in profound gratitude, saying, "It's over! It's over!

145

It's over! It's over!" ("The belief in separation is over!") I
adjusted my foot and continued the yoga series. The next
time I attended class, the teacher was standing behind me.
I was doing some other pose. She told me to adjust something and then she blurted out, "I love you!" Two straight
women in a packed yoga class at the gym experienced the
shared Love of God.

By our willingness to let the Holy Spirit show us what
God sees, Heaven shines through. A Course in Miracles calls
these moments "holy instants." The Course even says that
our lives can be a series of holy instants strung together. I
started seeing holy instants as "snack-sized" versions of the
revelation experience I had in the Indian restaurant. They
are breakthrough moments of Christ Vision. The more we
allow forgiveness to clear our upper subconscious level, the
more light can shine through. The holy instants come more
frequently. We experience shared, infinite, pure Love. They
motivate us to forgive whatever arises.

> "Vision will come to you at first in glimpses, but they will be
> enough to show you what is given you who see your brother
> sinless."
>
> ACIM.20. IX.67.

Toward the end of that year, I came to the part of A
Course in Miracles that answers the question "What is Christ?"
The section sparkled in a whole new way. It explains that
Christ is the only aspect of us that has any reality in Truth.
Christ is the Mind we share with one another and with our
Creator. The rest is dreams! It filled me with joy. Willingness
to recognize Christ in everyone is the readiness to awaken! I
started affirming the beautiful Truth every day:

AFFIRMATION:

"Christ is the only aspect of me that has any reality in Truth. Christ is the Mind that I share with everyone and with God. The rest is dreams."

I met a woman who thought she knew me, though we had never met. She started telling me my life story from her point of view as told to her by someone else. I was a character in her judgment story. She did not understand what she was talking about. In that moment, I thought, "This is amazing! It's is so obvious! My body's eyes and ears are showing bodies telling untrue stories! I am not who she thinks I am. She is not who I think she is. This is just an untrue story. We aren't our bodies or our stories." It was a perfectly designed lesson. I was so grateful that her unreal thoughts meant nothing to me.

Next, I saw a vision. It was like the scene in the movie *Cocoon* where the people unzip their bodies. She appeared as a flash of light. I was not reminding myself to visualize her as the light beyond her body. By the small opening of my willingness to remember what I did not know, I had a visual perception of her light. Simultaneously, the knowledge came into my heart-mind that the body is not the Source of Love. It was not an intellectual understanding but a heart knowing. The woman left and the healing stayed. Because this happened at a funeral, I needed the heart knowledge at that precise moment.

A short time before the funeral, I had asked the Holy Spirit to help me perceive death differently. I couldn't teach myself a different perception. But I trusted the Holy Spirit to respond to my willingness. I said this prayer: *"Take this from me and look upon it, judging it for me. Let me not see it as a sign of sin and death nor use it for destruction. Teach me how not to make of it an obstacle to peace, but let You use it for me to facilitate its coming"* (ACIM. 19.V.c.89).

Not only did I say the prayer, I *meant* it. The Holy Spirit arranged a perfect scenario that met my open mind. I learned by letting go and trusting my Inner Teacher, the Holy Spirit. Willingness is practical. My Teacher is showing me I have always been Christ and everyone has always been Christ. The Holy Spirit teaches us as soon as we are willing to learn.

The Holy Spirit will not force us to learn. When we turn to our Inner Teacher, the rewards are great. Now I enjoy going to yoga and go to class even though no one is telling me to go. When I was in high school, I got an "F" in gym class because I was not willing to go. Because of various concerts and music activities, I missed some classes. My gym teacher wanted me to make up gym after school, but I refused. So I failed gym and got my only "F" because I was not willing to learn about athletics. My gym teacher was Christ and so was I. It seems like it took many years for me to want to go to the gym and welcome the opportunity to recognize Christ.

In Reality, everyone that we have ever met or will ever meet has always been Christ. I have always been Christ. You have always been Christ. Everyone is Christ now, because of the Power of God. We are all Christ and the rest is dreams because God is our Source. If I deny the eternal Truth about myself, it does not change the Truth. Infinite Love is still the Truth about everyone because of God. I am so happy to remember that no mistaken thought I have ever imagined has changed what God created. Any unloving thought is just an unreal thought. *A Course in Miracles* says the past did not happen the way I remember it. In the past, everyone was Christ because Christ is Eternal. I have to practice remembering that dreams are unreal thoughts.

Accepting that everyone shares God's Mind has increased my willingness to admit I can't judge. Judgment is a false belief that I know everything. I do not. I don't want attack thoughts toward the Mind I share with God. By keeping Truth in my mind, I recognize my true safety. God is always with me, with you and with everybody. We are in God. This is helping me practice defenselessness. There is nothing to fear. Every moment is an opportunity to choose between weakness and the power of Christ within. We don't have to know what that will look like, because we don't.

Our Christ Self isn't attached to worldly outcomes. If you can't tell whether you are pushing something down or handing it over, ask yourself if you are willing to let go of outcome. Handing it over means letting go of outcome. Form does not last. Spirit is Eternal. In the healing moment, when an old fear has come up to our awareness, we can decide that we want to see it differently. We offer our willingness to have our *mind* corrected. (Whatever prayer works for you.) Give the fear to the Light.

I am so glad none of my unloving thoughts is real because I have to keep relinquishing them. When unreal thoughts come up, they are coming to go. It's part of the healing process. They weren't real in the first place because God didn't think them. God is Unconditional Love. Sometimes we can recognize our untrue thoughts by making mistakes. The Holy Spirit teaches by the reward system. By making mistakes and apologizing, I find out I'm safe even when I stumble. I can interpret the mistakes differently. They become learning experiences. What I learn is much more important than defending an unreal self. By practicing defenselessness, I am learning to accept the True Protection of the Holy Spirit. Sometimes I say, "Holy Spirit I am letting you be my One Defender." The Holy Spirit is already aware of the Truth; I am reminding myself of my willingness. "I'm jumping into your Loving Arms now...here I come!" It helps. When someone else tries to blame me for their mistakes and I don't defend, I find out Love really *is* the Answer to everything. This Unconditional Love Stuff works!

I used to push anger down and defend on the inside. Other people's approval was important to me, so I valued their unreal thoughts. It was not Love, but a defense against it. People pleasing is a way to use others to replace the Love of God as our Source. It never works and is inauthentic. So my Spiritual Teacher, the Holy Spirit, taught me how to set boundaries. I had to learn to be deeply honest with myself and others before I could practice defenselessness. People pleasing is a defense against the Truth. Boundaries *speak* the Truth. After I became grounded in the Love of God, The Plan gave me the opportunity to forgive myself for the years when I had tried to avoid my Source. Self Forgiveness Opportunity Delivery People came into my life showing me codependent behavior so I could see it was only a dream. They offered me the opportunity to see the Christ beyond their behavior. I had the chance to remember that in the past, the only thing that ever happened was Christ. The Self that God created as me had been Innocent and Whole all along, even when I didn't know it.

Imbedded within any earthly situation is the healing moment because it contains the opportunity to choose the Holy perception. Every situation is an opportunity for choosing peace. The Answer is the decision for Christ; the choice for joy, peace, love. By stepping back and letting the Holy Spirit show me the Truth in everyone and every situation, every day is Christmas, and I am surrounded by angels. The Universe is entirely invested in our remembering our Innocence, our Beauty, our Eternal Lovability. Thank You Angels, I see you unzipped, free, powerful and glorious.

We seal this chapter by sharing three "Oms."
Om…
Om…
Om…
Namaste.

PAY IT FORWARD

ON A MISSION FROM GOD

We are all here on a Mission from God. Our assignment is to extend unlimited Love. We have already been recruited and we are in the field. The Universal Happiness Plan has Called each of us and assigns us to specific areas, situations, and people. Part One of the assignment is the same for everyone—forgive. Part Two of the assignment is the same for everyone—extend the Love that is freed up by forgiveness. *A Course in Miracles* tells us, *"Miracles are natural expressions of total forgiveness. Through miracles, you affirm your acceptance of God's forgiveness by extending it to others"* (ACIM.1.21).

As we forgive, we are assigned to situations and relationships in which we can pay forward maximal Love, because we have forgiven. A Miracle is an expression of maximal Love. To receive the details of our assignments, we have to forgive. We can't hear the voice of fear and the Voice of Love at the same time. God is Love and *"Love holds no grievances"* (ACIM. Workbook.63). So, we can't represent Love with grievances in our heart-minds. Our unloving thoughts are resistance to fulfilling our function. Grievances are the refusal to accept our Mission. Our unloving thoughts are resistance to our relationship with God.

Situations are relationships. The True purpose of any relationship is love and joy because that is God's Will. In any worldly situation or relationship in which we are not experiencing joy and love, we are using the person or situation as an excuse to avoid God. Blaming the person or situation is yet another way to avoid love. If it could be their fault, we wouldn't have to look at our relationship with God. But there is no person or situation that has the power to separate us from God. Our True Self, Our Christ Mind, is forever One with boundless love and joy. When we are honest, we admit that we have used people and situations to distract ourselves from the one situation, the one relationship that never alters. We would rather misdirect our attention to fear and anger about a changing world than enter the Limitless Love we have now and forever.

Perhaps we'll open our hearts to ideas, situations, exciting new spiritual teachings. We'll try new things. *We're progressive!* What about opening our hearts to what has been inside all along? We are on the spiritual path because we *do* love God. What about admitting how *much* we love God—*really?* Are we willing to open to the *enormity* of that love? Does it seem risky? When we forgive, we recognize it's safe to love God without limitation.

As we progress on our spiritual journey, we lay aside the image we made of God as an external being that does our will in the world. Through forgiveness, we unlearn the meaning we gave to love. Our unloving thoughts are plucked from our minds with our permission. Sometimes we forget that our grievances are the unloving thoughts in our own minds. When we're busy justifying our unforgiveness storylines, we're forgetting *we* blocked God's Love from our awareness.

Even if someone else has a grievance toward *us*, it's still up to us to remain awake to love. I had to learn that. Don't enter the illusion of lovelessness. Love someone who is forgetting that they love me. I am responsible for my heart-mind. The Christ in them loves me. The Christ in the other person is the Self that God created. So even when it appears that someone else is not loving me, it's up to me to love and to listen for Guidance. Ask the Holy Spirit if there is anything for me to do. Usually, if someone is just projecting and it has nothing to do with me, my only job is to *not* enter fear. If there is a boundary to set, Spirit will advise me. If not, I often just send them love and wait it out. Be patient. Don't align to it. Bless them and it passes.

By bringing every unforgiving thought to the Spirit of Love within to be undone, we are giving our minds back to Love. This is the right use of our free will. Forgiveness heals our heart-minds as we turn back to God. We are reminding ourselves of what we *really* want. By our willingness to heal, we recognize that no one has ever hurt us. *The pains of our lives come from turning away from God.* That's what hurt. The belief that we could leave our Source. Whatever happened in the worldly storylines that we used as an excuse to keep OUR minds away from the eternal, boundless Love of God was just a wrong use of OUR mind.

By turning to the world to replace God as our source of love and joy, we find disappointment and heartbreak. The world is the realm of the ephemeral. Everything in the realm of the physical changes. Whenever we turned to the world for joy, love, or peace, it wasn't real. It was temporary and limited. *We have taught ourselves false lessons about love.* We have taught ourselves that love, joy and peace are limited and don't last. *This has led to a subliminal fear of God.*

Intellectually, we understand that God is Love. It's the *meaning* of love that has become distorted in our minds.

Forgiveness heals our relationship with God. As we forgive, we remind ourselves that there is no condemnation in Love. Our Christ Mind is in an eternal Right Relationship with God. Forgiveness puts us back into our Right Mind. We discover that our relationship with God is still intact. By our willingness to forgive, we accept the relationship that is waiting for us. As we turn back to the Essence of Love within, we learn there is no heartbreak in God. The Love of God is eternal. It's here now and forever. It's safe to turn back to Real Love. By forgiving—*really* forgiving—we find the Truth about Love.

When we stop using the world as a defense against Unlimited Love, the Real Love within our hearts rises into our awareness. We find our Whole Self. Now we Trust. We are ready for our Mission to serve Unlimited Love by sharing it in the world. We have become miracle-minded. Where we have forgiven, Universal Love can use us to represent the healed perspective. We didn't forgive just for us because we are never healed alone. The Voice of Love will show us where to go and what to do. All we have to do is follow.

Once, the weather forecasters predicted a big storm. For days, there were special reports with dire warnings. My inner voice predicted that someone would die during the storm. It was not a fear-based reaction to the storm. It was a persistent message. I tried to ignore the message. But it kept coming, just like the clouds. The local emergency management authorities called for residents of my area to evacuate. I packed the dog in the car and drove out of state to wait out the storm. (This was "B.C."—before cat.) On my way to Pennsylvania, funeral signs leapt out at me. The signs took on an extra dimension. The storm passed.

When I came home, I found out that a colleague had passed away during the storm (not because of it). Friends and colleagues invited me to the viewing and funeral. I had worked with this colleague on one project. We had a wonderful experience together, though it was not someone I knew well. Even though I kept getting prompts, I resisted going to the viewing. I told myself, "I don't go to viewings because we are not our bodies." As soon as I had the thought, I knew it was an excuse. It was the ego trying to sound spiritual. But I could discern the difference. When we commit to the Truth, we can see through the ego's tricks. Since we are not our bodies, it's not a problem to see one.

There was a yoga class at the same time as the service. I tried to use the yoga class as a reason to skip the funeral. The yoga studio emailed a notice cancelling the class. I got no support for my reluctance to follow the Divine prompts to attend the service. Every defense evaporated like the clouds after the storm. The signs were unmistakable. I had received the intuition. The Universal Plan cleared my calendar and excuses. Spirit had an assignment for me. As soon as I walked in to the church, I saw poster boards with photographs of the deceased person's life. The display included pictures of me with the woman from the time we collaborated. It was further confirmation that I was in the right place. It occurred to me that this woman and I had a lot in common on the physical level.

Inner Guidance directed me to sit down next to a specific person I had never met before. This person was very chatty and informed me of everything I needed to know for my assignment. While I was sitting there, I learned just how *much* I had in common with the woman who had passed. We had similar storylines. Both of us had used the world to defend against the Love of God in the same way and broken our own hearts. According to my informant, everyone at the service was shunning a particular person in attendance.

Everyone but me.

I had done my forgiveness work. I realized why I had been Called to the service. My part was to be *in* service of Unconditional Love. I was there to represent the Christ Mind of the person whose body was in the casket. Her body was not available to say, "You are completely forgiven. I see your Innocence. Nothing happened." We share the Universal Mind of Christ. So the Christ Mind used my body. It could not have used my body if I had not done my forgiveness work. But because I had, and because I had so much in common with the person on the physical level, I was tapped for the assignment. The Plan used me as an understudy.

All I had to do was shake a hand, look into someone's eyes and smile. This man was having a hard day. I had no judgment on him. I was there to deliver a silent message of blessing, "I see the Christ in You." My colleague and I collaborated again. We extended Love where it was needed. When we forgive, we are collaborating with Love by sharing it. When we follow Guidance, we are banding together with Divine Love in extending miracles.

By sharing love unconditionally, we learn the Truth about Love. All Real Love is maximal. All Real Love is the Love of God. The Love of God is Unconditional and maximal. It never changes and is the same in all situations. It is changeless. That's why all things are possible with God. When we are on a Mission from God, doing God's Will, sharing love, we recognize that everything is falling into place exactly according to God's Plan. We are not in charge of the plan; we carry out the Plan assigned to us.

We represent God's Love in the world.

Another time, The Plan sent me into a situation where I had a lot in common with someone whose body was not present. I had already done my forgiveness homework. This time, I didn't know the person whose body was not present. The Divine Plan shifted my plans around. I let my little plans fall away and followed the Bigger Plan that was unfolding. By the time I arrived at my destination, I recognized I was on an assignment. An informant filled me in upon arrival.

The Mission used people in three states and three countries to bring me to the situation in which I stood before people toward whom I had no judgment, only love. I was representing Christ. I did not have to *try* to represent Christ. Because I had done the forgiveness work in my own life, I saw the Truth about the people. The Holy Spirit had healed the illusions of guilt in my mind. I understood that the people in my past were innocent and these people were innocent. Any past hurt was caused by trying to use people and situations as a replacement for God. God can never be replaced as our Source. Our Innocence is intact. The Love of God has never been damaged or broken. When we accept Innocence, we are tapped by the Universe to pay it forward. Share the Truth.

That's why the Divine Plan used people in three states and three countries to have me stand before my assigned people in Unconditional Love. Those brothers and sisters in the three states and three countries were on a Mission from God, too. We are all on a Mission from God, should we decide to accept it. God only sees our Innocence. It is simple to follow the instructions of Unconditional Love through time and space when our minds are free.

There is no order of difficulty in miracles because none of our unloving thoughts is any more real than any other unloving thought. They are all just plain unreal. The Love that leads the way is Unlimited and so are we because Love is our Identity. We are all Called to Service by Eternal Love. God has Called you into the *Love Corps.* The benefits of this Mission include unlimited peace and joy. We are not in charge of our Mission. By allowing Love to clear our minds of untrue thoughts, we can serve Eternal Love. God gave the Holy Spirit the Mission to remove all self-imposed guilt from our minds, knowing that guilt is an untrue thought. *"It is impossible that this mission fail"* (ACIM 13.5.39). After all, it is a Mission from God. Only our willingness is necessary. It is how we forgive. We give the thoughts to the Holy Spirit to be undone. Giving those thoughts over is part one of our Mission.

Once our untrue thoughts are lifted from our minds, we are restored to our Right Mind. Our Right Minds are in direct communication with God because our Right Minds are One with God. Everyone's Right Mind is One with God. Our grievances are defenses against experiencing the Love of God. When we admit we were wrong about the meaning of love, we turn back to the Spirit of Everlasting Love. We find that there has never been a grievance in our relationship with God.

Now, we are ready to bless the world. What we forgive, we naturally bless. We are all needed. Your part is essential. Forgive wherever you are in this moment. You might be assigned as a stand-in for someone you don't know on the level of form. The miracles you extend will be perfectly designated for *your* journey. There is a part that only you can play. Your willingness will bless many people you may not even meet and you will never find out about. But it will always bless you.

Our forgiveness is our healing. Our forgiveness is sent forth to bless people whose current circumstances resemble those we formerly judged. We get to see our old storylines from the Christ point of view. That's how we know we are healed. It is a miracle. It's a testimony to the Love of God. There are Miracle workers blessing you every day. You will be given as much help as you are willing to receive. Your part will unfold in miraculous ways that you can't plan because you can't see the Whole. By allowing your mind to return to the wholeness of love, you will be available to *serve* the whole. You will be an instrument of blessing for the world.

Wait, listen and follow. You are on a Mission from God. You *cannot* fail because of Who is in Charge. Only your willingness is necessary and only what Unlimited Love would have you do is possible.

Thanks Be to God.
Amen

Epilogue

We all get to forgive ourselves. It's hilarious. One day, we realize *everything* has happened for this one purpose. *Accepting the Atonement;* working our spiritual practices; the books and classes lead to one place. A moment in time dawns on us when we *accept* the message of the Holy Spirit. The Voice of God has been singing through prophets, lovers and reggae singers. Suddenly, we *receive* the communication:

Love.
In a relaxed moment of Trust, we *accept.*

We remember the Love of God (Christ) is the Self we share with everyone, throughout time and space and beyond time and space. Every dog knows this. They have been teaching us unconditional love by demonstration for thirty-six thousand years. (We have been pretending we don't speak their woof language. Love really *is* patient.) Now our hearing is improving in direct proportion to our willingness.

Every morning, I gather via conference call with *Course* lovers from around the country. We pray, meditate and practice our Daily Lesson from the Workbook. One morning before the *A Course in Miracles* Daily Workbook Conference Call, I read the morning lesson. Inner Guidance instructed me to share my revelation experience as a guided meditation.

The lesson for that day (*"I am forever an effect of God."* Lesson 326) has the potential to:

1. Undo all resistance to the Love of God.
2. Trigger the ego's resistance to its undoing.

I chose option 1. The revelation experience had given me a peek beyond the veil. Only God can *give* revelation. But I could share my experience if Holy Spirit said so and The Voice for God within was prompting me. I prayed and asked that Holy Spirit guide the meditation through me. "I give my mouth to the Holy Spirit to use as a communication device for the Love of God."

My dear phone family and I joined our hearts and minds as I opened my mouth and let the words, feelings and energy flow. Afterward, we rejoiced and people thanked me. I heard my mouth saying, "Thank you for the opportunity to share with you. I had to forgive myself for coming back." As the words came out of my mouth, I knew this applied to every problem I ever appeared to encounter.

<blockquote>
I just knew.
(Thank you, mouth!)
</blockquote>

I *understood* what I had read and practiced for so many years. All of my perceived problems were projections of the subconscious fear that I had separated from God. The Holy Spirit knows that separation is not real. The Atonement is a perfect system. We give our fears to the aspect of Mind that doesn't believe in what is not true. The Holy Spirit forgives what never happened.

Earlier in the conference call, there was a discussion about the world. My mouth shared, "The world is a teaching a device, just like every situation and relationship. When we graduate from college, we don't burn down the school. We rejoice, accept our diploma and move forward." Inside my mind, I heard, "Sometimes we go back to the school as a teacher."

(Tail Wags.)

Thank you to my Teacher in all appearances—all people, all animals, earth, all situations throughout time and space, beyond time and space.

Yes, You.

Pamela Whitman teaches weekly classes on the Text of *A Course in Miracles* at Unity by the Shore in Neptune, New Jersey. She has led the daily national *A Course in Miracles Workbook Conference Call* since 2013. Pamela has been a frequent guest speaker at spiritual centers since 2005. Her "Miracle Revolution" and "Miracles" radio programs were broadcast on WLFR FM (91.7), Unity.FM and The Himalayan Broadcasting Company in Kathmandu, Nepal for ten years. Pamela hosts annual retreats for learning and relaxation. She began meditating in middle school and has practiced *A Course in Miracles* since 1989. She is an ordained minister of *A Course in Miracles* and a concert flutist with a degree in flute performance from The University of Michigan. She composes and records original music to promote inner peace.

www.pamelawhitman.com

ALSO FROM PAMELA WHITMAN:

Retreats and Events
pamelawhitman.com

Daily Conference Calls
acimconferencecalls.com

Music
pamelawhitmanandrichkurtz.com
pamelawhitman.com

For a Free Guided Meditation Download send an email to:
recordings@pamelawhitman.com
Subject Line: Free Download

CPSIA information can be obtained
at www.ICGtesting.com
Printed in the USA
BVHW041805250420
578480BV00010B/1695

9 781949 003338